Love Signs 1

Ca

For a further insight into what the future holds for you, CALL THE

The Secret of the Runes – see if the ancient spiritual tradition of the Rune Stones can answer your questions: **0891-111-666**

The Vision of the Cards – the 53 cards tell your fortune. Let us reveal their magic and see what the secret symbols of knowledge may hold in store for you: **0891-111-667**

Calls cost 39p per minute cheap rate, 49p per minute at all other times – prices correct at time of going to press

Sunday EXPRESS

Love Signs 1995

Cancer

22 June – 23 July

ARROW

First published in 1994

1 3 5 7 9 8 6 4 2

Copyright © Sarah Bartlett 1994

The moral rights of the author have been asserted

First published in the United Kingdom in 1994
by Vermilion Arrow
an imprint of Ebury Press
Random House, 20 Vauxhall Bridge Road,
London SW1V 2SA

Random House Australia (Pty) Limited
20 Alfred Street, Milsons Point, Sydney,
New South Wales 2061, Australia

Random House New Zealand Limited
18 Poland Road, Glenfield,
Auckland 10, New Zealand

Random House South Africa (Pty) Limited
PO Box 337, Bergvlei, 2012 South Africa

Random House UK Limited Reg. No. 954009

A CIP record for this title is available from the British Library

ISBN 009936617

Designed by Nigel Hazle
Typeset from author's disks by Clive Dorman & Co.
Printed and bound in Great Britain by
Cox & Wyman Ltd, Reading, Berks

Contents

Introduction

**Astrology is about _how_ we are,
not _why_ we are.**

This book aims to be a guide to what you might expect from people as lovers, partners and friends. It also gives you an insight into who you really are, and how others see you. The forecasts for October 1994 through to December 1995 reveal the _mood_ of the month for your Sun sign in the areas of love, emotions, sex, leisure and friendship. It will give you a fresh insight into getting the best out of your relationships for the months ahead. Keep your eyes on the stars and the stars in your eyes, and you won't go far wrong.

Astrology makes no claims to prophecy. It is only a reflection of human psychology: a mirror of us all and the paths we take.

Sun signs divide and generalise, no more or less than any other approach to our existence. They do show the basic qualities we have in common, the emotions and feelings and intellect that we all share and how we use our personal map of life. The map of life is in all of us, and every individual has his or her unique chart. Some areas of our personality are more prominent than others, like on the map of the world, where oceans and continents can be highlighted, or mountains or rivers. Sometimes we project different continents on to that map, other countries of feeling or mentality that are not highlighted on our own personal chart, but are highlighted in someone else.

There are so many other points involved in your natal chart that make you unique, so that when you read this book, remember that talking about a Virgo or a Scorpio can only be a beginning to knowing someone, the larger continents and oceans on their own psychological globe. These reactions and characteristics are not the only way a person will respond to situations. But Sun signs give guidance to the general way we feel, love and interact.

Unless your lover's Sun sign is severely afflicted, or has another more prominent sign in the natal chart, then he or she should be fairly consistent with the Sun sign image, though you may not recognise it instantly.

The sign rising over the horizon at the moment of birth has an equally powerful bearing on our psychological make-up. However, finding this out requires exact and detailed calculations, including certainty of time of birth. That is why our Sun sign is our primary pin-pointer on the map. You may not at first glance recognise yourself, because often your Sun sign reveals characteristics to which you don't want to admit!

As La Rochefoucauld put it so succinctly, 'Not all those who know their minds, know their hearts as well.'

The 12 Signs as Lovers and Partners

THE ARIES MAN

Aries is traditionally the first sign of the zodiac and that means that an Aries man comes first in everything. The Arien lover is bold, demanding, impulsive, and most certainly self-centred, and yet he will take risks in his relationships and in love. Because he cannot stand any kind of restriction to his freedom, you're more likely to find him hanging around motor races, rallies, outdoor activities rather than cutting cigar ends down the local pub. He's looking for adventure and, for the egotistic Ram, love-affairs are as much a challenge to him as hang-gliding.

One of the things that make him an exciting lover is his need to take chances. Romance to this impetuous man involves dragging you round the Himalayas at breathtaking speed and expecting you to eat vindaloo for lunch and dinner when you get back to the local Indian restaurant. He expects weekends in the camper in freezing winter with only each other to keep you warm! He needs a woman with guts both spirited and physically non-combustible to keep up with his vigorous lifestyle.

The arrogant Ram can fall in love easily, and impulsively, and if he genuinely believes that you are the answer to his dreams, he won't hesitate to become deeply involved. His sexual magnetism is tremendous, and he is so aware of his ability to attract women that he sometimes assumes that no one will reject him. This kind of arrogance can lead him into trouble, but his honest, no-nonsense approach always gets him back on top and he doesn't suffer from self-pity, ever.

What you must remember is that Arien hotheads are jealous Fire signs. It's quite all right for him to chat to other women, or even play a touch of harmless flirting, but for you to attempt even a smile at that charming colleague of his across the pub is fatal. In a crowded room you'll know the Aries man because he's the one with the self-confidence and the smile of a dare-devil lover. He might hastily introduce himself, arrogance and impulse working overtime to meet his challenger head-on. But if you crash, watch out for his honest vent to his feelings. It takes a lot to rile an Aries but, if you don't play fair and true, he won't let you forget it.

If you want a permanent relationship with him and can keep up with his energetic sex life you will be rewarded. But never forget that the Ram's egotism governs his need to satisfy himself first, and you second. But if you both can get over his self-centred approach to love and sex, for really he's always searching for an ideal, there is a lot of warmth and honest love waiting in his heart.

THE ARIES WOMAN

The Aries woman usually will want to be the boss in everything, including her love life. Because she is a Cardinal Fire sign, she knows intuitively what she wants. Some Aries girls will come straight to the point and pick you up, if you don't make the first move! Like her male equivalent, an Aries girl has great sexual magnetism, and if you're strong enough to take her on, you'll realise why her hot-headed vanity works.

Undoubtedly she will want to take over your whole life if you fall in with her hard-headed approach to relationships. She will always be ambitious for you, and for where she comes in your life. She is number one, and you will always be number two. If you can bear her egotistic pride then she will be the most loving and passionate partner, but she needs commitment, and she needs to be the centre of your world, or she'll dump you.

Another important consideration is that exclusivity is her *raison d'être*. And that will mean you. Once she's let you into the secret art of ram-shearing then she can get incredibly jealous if you stray out of the sheep pen. She may be a passionate lover, but that passion doesn't make her liberal about free love.

The Ram girl likes men to be young in outlook and appearance. If you've got the energy to go hang-gliding before lunch then you'll be her friend for life. But if you've got a gut hanging out over your trousers and would rather sit in front of the TV with a can of lager, forget having any relationship with her. She needs an energetic man both as a friend, to make impulsive trips and exciting journeys, but also in bed. There is a fire burning in her soul which doesn't need to be put out, it just needs rekindling from time to time. The adventure in her head and the energy in her blood keep her restlessly searching for the next impulsive trip on love. Love is beautiful if she can be the boss, and she can take control, but give her back as much as she puts into a relationship and you'll stay her adventure for life.

THE TAURUS MAN

The natural inclination of Mr Bull at dawn is to force himself out of the bed he cherishes so much. But that's the only bit of forcing he'll do, particularly in any relationship. If he wants you then *you* have to be the one to chase him, but the move will be welcomed. A Taurean male won't actually make many advances and stubbornly waits for those who are worthy of his incredible sensual attention to come running.

For all this laid-back man-appeal it may appear that sex means little to him. But actually that's the catch. The Taurean male's quite seething sexuality, once unleashed on an unsuspecting female who decides to consider him as her partner, can be quite overtly bestial.

He thinks as highly of his body as he does of the next meal or the next bath. The Bull loves the pleasures and luxuries of life and is essentially an implacable part of the earth, intensely sensual, and dependable. He is an Earth sign whose energy and sexual drive originates from all that natural organic goodness that ironically he rarely eats.

There's actually something quite elusive about Taureans. You can never quite fathom out where they've come from, or really exactly where they are going to, probably because they really have no idea, nor care about it themselves. This is why it can take a long time to form a deep relationship with a Bull. If you do get past the horns, this affair could be for life. The placid Bull needs gentle handling, both emotionally and sexually. The trouble is that Mr Bull is often very blind to his own compatibility ratings. He is lured by, and hopelessly attracted to, Fire and Air signs. The Taurean man often gets tangled up with the Airy intellect or impulsive brainstorming of these very opposite types from him. He just can't keep up with the mind-bending improvisation that these signs so naturally use to charm their way through life.

The Taurus man is warm-hearted and affectionate, and he is intensely passionate. But he is a lover of the pleasures of life, a hedonist in every self-indulgence, and every luxury. Sex is a good, basic pleasure which he enjoys as part of a deep and erotic relationship. If after a heavy night of wining and dining he prefers to sleep off the last glass of brandy rather than spend the night with you, it's not that he's selfish, just that he forgot you for a while. After all, there are other sensual things in his life apart from sex, had you forgotten that?

THE TAURUS WOMAN

It's hard to imagine the placid, reliable, earth mother as a hard-edged Bull, but there is a side to her which might have been overlooked! A Taurean female takes a long time to decide if you are worthy of her passion, yet she has the power and the guts actually to initiate the first move in a relationship and should never be underestimated. A bossy girl needs careful handling, and because she is strong-minded and loyal she needs first-class devotion in return.

The Bull lady bears little resemblance to bovine sensuality except for an occasional grumbling temper and a geyser of bubbling anger when she gets overheated by resentment. Pouts grow on a female Taurean's lips very easily. Jealousy is uncommon, but possessiveness is. Her placid, controlled approach to your relationship is her self-protection, her magic eye. She has to impress and be impressed, which is why she often gets tangled up with men with a big cheque book. She likes the sound of champagne corks flying and the permanence of marriage.

Sensuality is the Taurean girl's be-all and end-all. It could be the summer rain pattering on your back as you kiss beneath an umbrella, or making love in the pine forest or beside the babbling stream. She's a creature of the outdoors, of closeness to nature and filling her senses with tastes, sounds and touch.

Venus in cowhide will be delighted equally whether she's having sex, floating in a silky warm ocean, eating pizzas at three in the morning, or cooking you both a cordon bleu breakfast in a tent. Sex is not to be taken lightly and she can get quite prudish with women who are apparent flirts or downright promiscuous. Convinced that a good emotional and sexual relationship is the answer to fulfilment, she might well confide her Mother Earth instincts to you one warm night.

The awkward and niggling little word 'possession' might create a spot of tension but, if you're willing to be a mate for life, or at least more permanent than the fading perfume on her skin, you will have to take sex and love as seriously as she does. If you can offer her honesty and maybe a sound financial future, a superb champagne dinner or a night listening to the owls in the woods, then she will be impressed enough to let you through her tough, resilient Bull-skin.

This girl needs both erotic and sensual communication, a man who can give her a down-to-earth lifestyle and a really warm heart. But make sure you've got the stamina and nerve to accept her blatant honesty if she decides to reject you!

THE GEMINI MAN

The highly versatile, spontaneous and amusing Gemini man is always ready for any mental and sexual challenge. He lives in the air, rather than flat-footed on the ground. Passion and sensuality are a rarity in his love life, for he is the catalyst of communication. The will o' the wisp is inquisitive, and like a child he will want to play games, will move through your life like a shooting star, and never make promises about tomorrow. He is privileged with a youthful appearance and a youthful approach to life. But emotionally, Gemini men rarely let you into their space, in fact they can often seem very cold, in the air, out of their heads and hardly ever in their hearts.

The second problem with which you have to wrestle is that there are always at least two personalities to cope with in one guise. This can be quite alarming when you wake up in the morning with a total stranger, not the man you thought you spent the night with! The seductive and alluring man of the late evening can turn into the clown at breakfast, and never be prepared to stay for lunch. The cherub-like Botticelli twins are actually not so much twins as a couple of conmen, both trying to outwit the other. Because of the mental struggle of trying to figure out his own identity, a Gemini male needs variety and change in his life. This means that he is often promiscuous, often marries at least twice and always wants two of everything. He has this uncanny ability and agility to be all types of lovers imaginable because role-playing stops him from ever being truly himself. And actually he really doesn't know who he is himself.

The double-lover enjoys the company and friendship of females just as much as any intimate physical relationship. Sexually he is the least chauvinistic of the star signs, and would rather spend the evening discussing the world and sipping champagne with you than be down the pub with the boys. He prefers to move on, to change partners, to try out new experiences, whatever forecast is in the wind, and to leave the fog of commitment and emotion far behind him.

If you can give him fun and variety he might even hang around to breathe your kind of fresh air. The Gemini man is often likened to Peter Pan, but if you ask any girl who's been involved with the Twins, she'll say, 'Sure, he reminded me of Peter Pan; but wasn't he like all those lost boys too?'.

THE GEMINI WOMAN

The female twins sparkle at parties, vibrating among other women who would rather keep cool and mysterious and watch this flirting charmer draw men to her like junkies to a fix. That's why a distortion of the facts has arisen and Miss Gemini has been dubbed two-faced in love, and a hypocrite in bed. So it's about time the true nature of this multi-faceted woman was revealed!

They seek out and need constant change in both their social lives and their love lives, not to mention their careers and their home life. Miss Fickle can jump headlong from the trivial to the profound in a split second because she's more interested in actual cleverness than the truth. She may have two or more faces, but they are all genuine in her own eyes, and in her own pretty head. Gemini girls are adept at role-playing, from switching from heaven to earth. Give them a character, a *femme fatale*, an innocent virgin, a career woman, you name it, they can play it. If you can keep up with their flighty, pacey, restless way of life, then you'll have more than one woman to keep you company at bedtime.

Apart from the thousand faces that Gemini women possess they are also known to be incredible flirts. It's not so much that she's particularly infatuated with you, it's more likely that she wants to play the game, drink her way through a bottle of champagne and then go home to sleep off the mental exhaustion of it all. She needs a lot of sleep, but a Gemini woman is more likely than any other sign to prefer to sit up all night discussing the latest philosophy, or the latest painting in your collection, or the books on your shelf.

She makes vague attachments, and loves socialising, but very rarely makes deep friendships, particularly with her own sex. Miss Fickle prefers the company of men to women and would rather be one of the boys at the office.

Gregarious girls meet a lot of blokes, so Gemini woman will be well surrounded by a choice selection. But remember, she's attracted to appearances rather than to depth of emotions. She is capable of persuading herself you're the love of her life. Being in love is easy if you talk yourself into it. Why, then, you can talk yourself out of it again when it takes your fancy, or another man does! (By the way, a Gemini girl's heart is a pretty cold place to penetrate, but if you ever get through the surface with your ice-pick at least you take pleasure in knowing that you will be remembered in her heart for being the only man that ever made it!)

The Jekyll girl often has affairs with younger men because she feels safer; commitment won't be spread across the bed with the Sunday papers at eleven in the morning after a night of hot passion. The marmalade men, the electric shavers and the city bods who need slippers and pipe won't attract her. She is capable of finding something fascinating and appealing in practically all men, but that doesn't mean it will last more than the second that it takes for her to change their mind, instantly! Enjoying sex isn't the answer to her dreams, only another dream can have that solution. And you can't stay her dream for ever – or can you?

THE CANCER MAN

The Cancerian man is home-loving, gentle and sincere. He responds deeply to life and to every change in emotion or feelings around him. His goodness far excels his weaker, depressive side which can get unbearable and drown an affair in melancholy. His moods can be touchy, he can be as snappy as an alligator and he takes everything too personally, fearing rejection. Yet on the surface he will play the extrovert, be flirtatious, the lunatic everyone loves at the all-night party.

A Crab man is overly sentimental. He will take a long time to pluck up enough courage to phone you, until he is sure in his Crab-like way he can move in for love. Don't forget, Crabs move sideways, stay in their shells and guard themselves ferociously with giant claws.

He might seem mildly indifferent: playing guessing games about his true motives with you when he first takes you out to dinner.

He loves food, and if you offer him breakfast in bed he might just agree to scrambling the eggs himself. This man needs smothering with affection, and sexually can be languid and lazy when it suits him, especially once he feels secure in a relationship. Typical of Water signs, he feeds on gentle rhythms, quiet arousal and delicate love-making.

Don't ever mention your past boyfriends because he will see vivid mental movies about where you have been, and who you have been with. Cancerians are very possessive, and if you mention ex-partners, he will wallow in self-pity for days.

Don't ever look at anyone once you're married. You are collected, part of his acquisitions and his very personal private collection.

Cancer men hide out in the dark corners of pubs, or at the edge of the in-crowd. If they use their extrovert shell to cover up their weaker personality they can be awkward to spot. Sometimes they hover in the wings, hiding from possible failure, appearing as confident and glib as any fire sign. But around the full moon you can usually spot them when they become touchy and moody, not at all like any Fire sign!

The Crab is easily flattered, and often gullible in the face of a strong protective, woman. He has a cheeky, little-boy-lost appeal that he takes to parties in his search for the perfect soul-mate, and he needs one desperately for all his apparent self-confidence and arrogant manner. It's misleading. Beneath that gregarious shell is a soft heart. There will only ever be one woman at a time for a Cancerian man – at least you can be assured of that.

THE CANCER WOMAN

When you meet the Cancer woman you will immediately know that you have met the most female of all females. The Yin is intense, explosive, warm and genuine, the genie of the zodiac, the sensitive soul, the Moon disabled by love and emotion. You have nothing to fear, except yourself, and the changeability of her deep and dark side. The dark side of the Moon waits for you. Do not disappoint her for the woman with whom you have just become infatuated is the past-mistress of love and romance.

Cancer ladies are easily flattered and at their worst are unstable. Preparation for a life of swaying moods, indistinct emotions and powerful sensitivity have adapted this dippy bird to seek attention and seek out sympathy from a nice guy, one she hopes will have a larger cheque book than her own.

She is protective, gentle, highly intuitive and reflective of others' moods. Yet like the Moon she sways, changing the light of the night from that pale ghostly shadowland to human and loony laughter. A bit touched, a bit sad, occasionally glad, Moon birds need close friends, domesticity and a strong, tender man to support them.

You can only get so close to a Moon bird. She has this intense fear of being opened up like a clam. The big problem for her is that if she doesn't open up then you might reject her like the bad mussels in the cooking pot that get tossed in the bin. Frankly, the Cancerian girl needs a permanent, stable relationship with someone who won't get twisted and confused every time she sulks or goes loopy in the Full Moon. You've been introduced to an apparently hard, tough, thick-skinned woman in the crowd. It really seems unlikely that someone so extrovert and resilient could be reduced to tears by a slight put-down. But she can! She's an extrovert/introvert, a manic depressive and a bundle of fun when she's on one of her highs. She can be downright rude and criticise everything about you from your haircut to your taste in underwear but she won't survive an in-depth dissection of her own deeper and often weaker character. Cancer women will never make the first move, because they sincerely cannot cope with rejection.

A word of warning. This lady can get her claws into you quicker and more deviously than any other Crab this side of the Moon. The claws of a Crab can grab you and, pincer-like, they'll clutch at your heart and possessively monopolise you, as she possesses her books, her kitchen memorabilia and her dog.

Her imagination sizzles in bed, like throwing water on fire. But she needs emotional and sensual fulfilment, a physical experience that will change as easily as her moods. Cancerian ladies don't take to athletic body-building, or get obsessed about their weight, but they will make or break the sexual traditions if it means pleasing the one man they really want to impress.

THE LEO MAN

The Leo man is known for his magnanimous nature and his warm and generous heart. But he is also a prowler, one of the more sexually active signs of the zodiac. Like Capricorn and Scorpio he is motivated by power. The subtle difference is that Leo assumes success in everything he does, particularly when it involves relationships and love. He can't bear the thought of rejection so he never even thinks about it. That's why he blazes his way through life, and that is how he wins.

For all his flash behaviour the tom-cat is actually in need of a lot of stroking. He falls in love easily, but it will often be subconsciously motivated by the desire to impress his companion. The Cat is a show-cat, wherever and whoever he is with. Leos have dramatic tastes, extrovert and extravagant desires, unnerving energy and yet he is so self-opinionated that he can be intolerably conceited and inflexible.

They need to be in the headlines and to draw attention to themselves, so the Leo lover will look for the sort of woman who can enhance his Mogul image and taste for hedonistic delights.

If you're good-looking, independent, can hold your own and be part of his show, then he'll fall in love with you on sight. The one thing you have to remember is that the golden boy, for all his showiness, is actually not very brave. He doesn't take risks like an Arien or Sagittarian, and he generally takes more care about who he gets involved with to avoid hurting his delicate pride. His emotions are fiery, but his judgment is cautious.

For long-term commitment, a Leo will be willing to take the risk only if he gets as much attention as he believes he deserves.

He will have mastered all the techniques of high performance love-making. That is something that he can really impress you with. But while you're enthralled by his energetic love and sexuality, remember that he likes to play the Tom-and-Jerry game. Mostly he prefers to be Tom, but even Tom needs a lot of affection and warmth, for all his boasting conceit. Cold, unresponsive girls can make him temporarily impotent and turn that organised high-flyer to anger; and that's when he can really leave a trail of charred hearts!

THE LEO WOMAN

The Cat woman is one of those girls who is always surrounded by men at social events. She will insist on being the centre of attention at all parties, which is one of the reasons she always organises them. The Leo girl also assumes she will be the nucleus and hotbed in any relationship and, for her, relationships need to be warm, affectionate and full of physical expressions of love. Bear-hugs, stroking her wild hair as if she is a pussy-cat are all gestures that show how she is adored. And she needs that very badly. This naturally vivacious, clever Cat finds men drawn to her like mosquitoes to blood.

This very sexual Cat can at times be overpowering and overdramatic, but her magnetic personality always catches the limelight.

Leo was born to lead, and not to follow. If you are strong enough to challenge her, then she may play the role of a sweet innocent for a while. But if she's not the starring role in your life then the loud, extravagant will of her ego will come hurtling out to confront you. And a Leo in full temper and voice is a pretty frightening Big Cat!

Her vanity irritates other women and attracts many men, and she can be arrogant and incredibly stubborn. She is self-opinionated, but she is also generous and compassionate, able to create the kind of atmosphere in the bedroom fit for the most sensual and seductive love-making imaginable!

If you can keep up with her energy and delight in passionate and exciting sex, then she might decide to make you a permanent fixture. The Cat woman will scratch for her independence, and won't sacrifice her career or freedom for many men. Although she will flirt her way through a boardroom of old fogeys to assure success in her career, you will have to trust her integrity.

Flatter her and she'll let you closer. Her vanity and her magnetic personality are, ironically, her weakness. But with respect and belief in a Leo woman you can be assured of a loyal and true partner. Never try to control her or play ego games. She needs a strong man who will pamper her; give her the world and in return she'll give you everything back. Attention-getting, and attention-seeking go together, so be prepared for the occasional mild flirtations when she's out at her business lunches, or career parties. If she weren't the star of the show someone else would be, and she really doesn't want anyone else to take that leading part away from her.

THE VIRGO MAN

If anyone could be more accurate, more perfect at time-keeping than a quartz watch, then it would have to be the Virgo man. He is the precision master, the careful and discriminating quiet one in the corner of the bar, who will drink exactly the same amount of alcohol every visit, and who knows precisely the health advantages of wine and the mortality rate of heavy drinkers. This neat and tidy man often pulls weights down the gym rather than girls, and worries about his digestion and whether he should be celibate.

The Virgo man finds warm, emotional relationships difficult, and yet he seeks out quality and the perfect woman. He analyses sex and relationships with the meticulous interest of a stamp-collector. You see, Virgo men don't really need anyone else in their lives. They often panic about their lack of passion, and then devote an awful lot of time worrying about it. (Virgos are constantly fretting about life.) Mr Precision sometimes falls in love with the logic of a relationship, with the actual methodology of it all, but very rarely is deep and genuine emotion involved.

Virgo men have this thing about purity. Not that they are chaste and virginal, but they will search for the purist form of experience and will often sublimate passion for neutrality. This is why if you're not near perfect in his eyes you'll be rejected before he even attempts to test you out. Sex can be a pure and impeccable experience for a Virgo with a girl in mint condition and the right motivation. But is there any life in his soul, any passion or warmth in that apparent cold and solitary physique?

He is very attractive to women because he appears to be a challenge. If you get past that cold shoulder there might just be a sensual, sensational warm heart. He has a heart, but it's as invulnerable as his emotions. On the surface he is the perfect lover and can perform like Don Juan. He is the sexual technocrat of the zodiac. If you can put up with his dissection of your personality, if you like a distant lover and a punctual friend, a lover who is dextrous but unemotional, he might make one of the better permanent relationships. But he compartmentalises life: the past stays the past, the future the future. He carries little sentimental or emotional baggage with him. It's tidier, isn't it?

If you finally get through the cold earth that buries this man you'll find a faithful lover. He's not exactly a bundle of laughs, but the strong silent type who once he's found his perfect partner will never, ever look at another woman again.

23

THE VIRGO WOMAN

The Virgo girl is quiet, self-aware and keeps her eyes firmly pinned on anything that might remotely interfere with her calculated plans for life. This includes her personal relationships which are as critically analysed and subjected to meticulous scrutiny as if she were conducting a witch hunt or a scientific experiment.

Miss Virgo is not only critical of herself, she is acutely critical of others. She nit-picks rather than knits, and can really infuriate you with her constant reminder that you have a speck of dandruff, or your tie is wonky. She believes that she knows best, and this confident mental sharpness affects all her personal and sexual relationships.

She expects tidiness and perfection around her which includes an organised pristine relationship with her ideal man. The Virgo girl can lack real human warmth at her worst and, because she is such a worrier, even sex can become a chore, and your performance tainted with imaginary faults.

But a Virgo girl loves romance: the first innocent kiss or the love-letters scribbled from a stranger. She can become infatuated with someone over the phone, or by the pure physical beauty in a man. She loves sentiment and delicate love-making. An Interflora sign will make her weep and she's nuts about soppy films, as long as no one is with her when she watches them. If you are too dominant a partner she can become frigid just to suit herself. Coldness is natural to her.

Perfection is wasted on talentless men and she will often be fatally attracted to opposite dreamy types, escapist musicians and artists who, although they fulfil her romantic fantasy, lead her to find fault with every work of art or creation they perform. The Virgo girl is dedicated to pursuing happiness, and her strength is to be able to be both obsessively practical and ridiculously romantic, because love is the purist form of analysis.

Sex will be a delight to her if you keep it light and

emotionless, but don't ever be late for a date, or her time-keeping will start clocking you in and out of her bed. She'll never be unfaithful, it's not in her nature. But if you can't enflame that spark of sexuality out of her ice-box she will quite coldly and mercilessly look for it elsewhere. The modest, clever and cautious Virgo girl will be the most affectionate and prudent partner if you can accept her perfectionism. She might decide you're her ideal and throw a party; but she'll stay in the kitchen and worry about the spilled punch. Someone has to haven't they?

THE LIBRA MAN

Libra is the go-between of the zodiac – the man who can be active or passive, will be laid-back, indecisive and fluctuate between love and sex in his head, easy-going, well mannered and everybody's friend. Doesn't that sound like the sort of man you would love to have around? Someone with wit and humour, who curves through life rather than angles through it? He is essentially a relaxed man who is fair and lovely about the world and naturally charming with every female he meets.

He needs harmony, beauty and idealistic truth in his life. For him, life has to fulfil dreams of romance, particularly when love and sex are involved. But this is where he gets confused. Not because he's a soppy sentimentalist, far from it, but because he thinks sex is love and love is sex. You just can't have one without the other, it wouldn't be fair.

This sociable man needs and demands a lot of friends of both sexes. If you get involved with a Libra be prepared to tolerate all the other female friends he spoils. Some of them may even be ex-lovers that he hasn't quite decided whether to see again or not.

But there are times when a Libran won't be forced into making a decision at all and, when it comes to any conflict, emotional or physical, he would rather walk out than fight. The eternal problem for Librans is *not* making a decision. What bugs him is why he has to make a choice about commitment in his relationship, because essentially he hates to reject anything, and that mostly includes his freedom.

He wants the best of both worlds, if he can get it, and flirting his way through life enables him to meet many women, and maybe, just maybe, he'll find the girl of his dreams. He often gets led astray by strong, glamorous females. He can fall instantly in love, but he falls in love with the essence of the affair, rather than the girl. The face value of the romance is all that matters to him initially.

Like Gemini the Ping Pong man is attracted to the appearance of life, not any underlying spiritual meaning.

He's a romantic and a balloon-seller of ideals, releasing them on a windy day to see if they fly alone. He loves the romance of sex, the caresses, the body language, the first meetings. Sexually his head rules his body. His approach is one of airy, cloudless skies and often a languid, lazy love-making. But his soaring passion is an insubstantial mental process, and he often has trouble 'being there' with you.

This sexual egalitarian is a wonderful lover and romantic, but remember, he can fall out of love as easily as he fell into it!

THE LIBRA WOMAN

What if you meet a Libran woman surrounded by a group of adoring friends and she decided you were the most attractive, exciting man in the room? You invite her to dinner and she falls in love with your eyes and your hair and immediately and uncharacteristically accepts the date. An hour later the chances are she'll change her mind, or sweetly point out that actually she is with Tom, an old flame, and really she can't accept because they are already going down the pub that night. What if Tom got upset?

And what if Tom really was the man of her life, the ideal she's searching for? And then what if she rejects your offer and you don't make another? This is the terrible dilemma for a Libran woman.

She is lovely, perfectly lovely. Attractive, gregarious, articulate, spirited and independent. A real woman but with a tough head and a strong heart. She's mentally alert and logical about life like any Air sign, but she really hates to reject anything, or anyone. And making decisions just means not having the best of both worlds, doesn't it?

Libran women have deliberately charming smiles which they can turn on when it suits them, to show how wonderfully feminine they can be. But the logical intensity of her mental gymnastics can be slightly off-putting if your intentions are of a deeper or more physical need.

She needs honesty, beauty and truth around her, no heavy emotion and no remorse. She'll cheer you up when you're down, brighten your life with her sparkling humour and will thoroughly enjoy sexual pleasure and hedonistic delights. Don't be a spoilsport or a worm, and if you can't find your way out of a paper bag then you're not her kind of man.

She'll love you for ever if you are her mental equal and her physical mirror image. But remember, this girl can be led astray by beauty and by the idea of love. Like her male counterpart, she can fall in love with the affair before she knows who you are. She'll listen to your opinions about politics, point out her own, then with equal fairness spout everyone else's point of view. That's why getting close to her heart can take a long time. She talks a lot, and she talks for everyone. Can you really find her beneath all those fair judgments?

THE SCORPIO MAN

Apart from a snake or a hypnotist, a Scorpio man has the best chance of fixing his penetrating eyes upon the one he loves or lusts and capturing her. No matter how hard you resist if he gets it in his head to seduce you, this man will hypnotise you before you've got back from the bar with your glass of white wine.

Like any insect, the Scorpio male has the ability to rattle and repel. You can meet him at the standard office party and find him offensive and unnerving, disagree with him about every subject under the sun, but he'll have you, and there's nothing you can do about it!

In Yoga, Kundalini is the serpent who lives at the base of our spine and is awakened upon sexual arousal. Any true Scorpio male's Kundalini is on permanent red-alert. To him sex and love are the whole meaning of life and the answer to every emotion. His attraction to women is motivated by his obsession for finding the truth, and often he falls prey to his own intentions by a touch too much promiscuity. The trouble is Scorpios actually need long-term and stable relationships. But the man is dangerous if you are on his hit-list. He'll pursue you secretively at first. If you find you are the chosen one he can also take over your whole existence.

Sometimes Scorpio will adore you until he actually destroys love, and you, in his mind and soul. It's the regenerative process of the Pluto passion, so you might as well enjoy the attention and the ecstasy while you can before he kills the love he has created.

His jealousy is intense. He lives and breathes every emotion, and with it love. He'll surprise you with spicy and secret rendezvous. In bed he'll be the connoisseur of all things sexual and emotional. He will want sex to be a symbolic, esoteric experience that sometimes falls close to obsession. Sex is big business to him and he can justifiably prove it with his reputation of a discreet but highly dangerous lover. But he has incredibly high standards and you must be spotless, almost virginal. The Scorpio male wants all or nothing, and the longer your mystery is prolonged the more intense the turn-on he gets.

You have to be emotionally and mentally strong to have

a relationship with this man. If you think you can handle him, can bear the shock when his eyes start to penetrate another victim's heart across the room, beware! This man is powerful. A boa constrictor takes a very long time to kill its prey – by gently squeezing the life out of it; until it can breathe no more.

THE SCORPIO WOMAN

The powerful seductress of the zodiac takes life seriously, too seriously at times. When she first sets eyes on you she will want to dominate you both physically and emotionally. Scorpio girls have an intuitive awareness of their sexual magnetism and, like sparks of static electricity, you will feel her presence in the room, whether you've met the haunting gaze of her eyes or not.

Watch out when she's about, for this dark, deeply motivated lady can play any charming role, any teasing subtle game that will make you think you are in control, not her.

If she could, the female snake would have been born a man, but as she has to bear the physical weakness of woman, she is more like the Medusa's head than one serpent, and more like a dozen Plutonian meteorites than a simple solitary moon.

For a Water sign she gives a pretty good impression of a Fiery one. Playing the *femme fatale* is easy for she creates subtle intrigue, the mystery and enigmatic power of a genie or a sorcerer. She can be hot and dominating one minute, then an emotional wreck the next. She'll hate voraciously and she'll love passionately. Whatever emotion she feels, she feels with intensity.

If she falls in love with you it will, for that moment, at least be for ever. Playing games with her is fatal, and if you start thinking the relationship should remain casual and lighthearted you might get a shock when she starts calling you on the phone in the middle of the night with tears, threats and demands.

Strength in a man is the Scorpio girl's weakness. The more independent, the more ambitious you are, the more she will love you. Sex and love are like a parasite and its host; without one you can't have the other. Remember, she takes her relationships very seriously and will sacrifice you for another if it means the total fulfilment of her soul.

Power is crucial to her existence and she won't be thwarted. Her strength of character is admirable, and her sexuality is so intense that it could take a lifetime really to know her. Secrets are big words for Scorpio girls, so make sure you have plenty, but keep her own mystery to yourself.

THE SAGITTARIUS MAN

The Archer is born altruistic, bold and voracious. It seems that he has the spirit and the morals of an Angel but watch out, the legendary bowman is more likely to have the soul of a gambler and the morals of a sexual extortionist. With unnerving blind faith and the optimism of Don Quixote this happy-go-lucky man wins his way through life and relationships like a trail of fiery stars. His honest and blunt admission for loving women make him the sort of guy that other men hate and women adore. It's not the egotistic vanity of an Aries, nor the power-driven motivation of a Leo; this Fire sign is genuinely convinced that this is the way things are. He can't help it if he was born beautiful, can he?

He's honest and open about himself, doesn't pretend to be something that he's not, and certainly lets you know if he's had enough of your company. He flirts easily, is really everybody's friend and is lighthearted and easy about life and women.

No strings and no commitments make this man's sense of freedom and need for a blank cheque in personal relationships sacrosanct.

Often the Archer looks for adventure, sexual or otherwise, as long as he can maintain his buccaneering spirit. That is why Sagittarians often resort to casual relationships to make sure there is nothing to stop their capricious wanderings. Meeting challenges head-on is the way the Archer travels through life and love. He responds to the thrill of the chase, of a woman who is hard to pick up. But he is idealistic and if you live up to his high standards he has the uncanny ability to know exactly how things are going to work out with you. If the Archer actually agrees to make an arrangement to meet you the following week and the stars are in his eyes as well as yours, you might think you had instigated the wonderful moment. But Sagittarians have this knack of making you think big, and sharing their expansive nature.

Like the other Fire signs, Sagittarians need outdoor activities and an extrovert lifestyle. If you can keep up with his active and quite fast-paced life he might consider you to be the pal he's looking for. Sex isn't everything to a Sagittarian, he needs someone to play mental and physical games too. He needs an inventive sex life, and his moods can range from passionate and fiery to warm and playful. Sex is fun, not a deep emotional experience.

So don't ever get soppy about him, he really doesn't like the kind of woman who hangs around like a lost doll, or who hasn't a life of her own. The Archer needs someone who is never possessive and rarely jealous, though on occasions he can be.

Watch out for the hailstones though, the Sagittarian can flash in and out of your life like a magnetic storm to avoid those rainclouds of commitment. But if he's convinced you're as free and easy, as unemotional and as unpossessive as he is, then maybe he'll forget about his unreliable and irresponsible attitude to life, and settle for permanent free love. That paradox is what he really wants.

THE SAGITTARIUS WOMAN

The outspoken Archer woman will insist on letting you know if you don't match up to her ideal, and she'll also pull your ideas apart with frank and brutal honesty which, to the uninitiated, can be a cultural shock. She lives independently and is always happier if her freedom isn't curtailed. Her honesty is genuine but it can sometimes cut through your heart like a butter knife, particularly as she's one of the most vivacious, amusing and popular females.

She prefers the company of men in any social setting and openly flirts in a rather innocent and childlike way. Like her Geminian opposite sign, she has no need for emotional depth to her relationships and prefers the surface attractions, the moles and wrinkles of appearances, rather than the viscera of human emotion. Friendship and companionship are more important than close emotional ties, and often platonic relationships with men and keeping friendly with ex-lovers is the easiest way to maintain her freedom and ensure an easy-going existence.

She can be so frank, that discussing her ex-boyfriends' intimate inclinations can sound like boasting to your ear, when she was only just letting you know how absurd she finds the whole sexual game. She doesn't mean to hurt anyone, never means to upset or put down a friend, and will end up confused and embarrassed by her own big mouth.

But an Archer girl's optimism spreads through her life and into her partner's with the ease of ripe brie. To be so confident, to be so sure that a relationship will work as long as she has her freedom, is a bonus to any partnership.

Communicating inner emotions and deeper tensions is not part of her vocabulary and that's why she often confuses love with casual friendship. Sex is also not to be confused with love, and she can have a strong physical relationship with a man and just be good friends. Being a pal is easier, doesn't lead to commitments, to arrangements, and traps like that big word 'love' always seems to do. If she's kept you up all night at a dinner-party, played the life and soul, flirted with your dad, and hardly noticed your jealousy, don't expect her to apologise. Her mind is set, and her morals are high, but she does like to have fun, her own way. If you want her to do anything, always ask nicely, never order her or tell her. She won't be bossed, in public or in private, or in bed.

Don't trap this incurable romantic. Don't question her, and you'll find her free love is all for you!

THE CAPRICORN MAN

The Capricorn male is often likened to that goaty god, Pan. On the surface Pan may be a dour, apparently bloody-minded hard-liner, but somewhere underneath it all you might find some true warmth and a consistently easy-going nature.

Capricorns are often conventional and rarely let themselves slip into any gear other than the one they have selected. In relationships with women they need to be in control. Even a power-mad Pan's chaos is controlled. In the wild abandon of infatuation his feelings and emotions are held from the precipice of freedom. He will be in charge of his destiny and yours, if you so much as show any inkling of desire for him.

He admires women who can coax him out of his stuffy Goat ways. But he also likes women who are ambitious for him too. Can this bedrock of society really rock the sexual and emotional bed? If he never deviates from his own tethering circle, will he ever have fun? A few women can release him from his rope of cold love. His inner nature often mellows as he ages, and oddly enough the paradox of this man is that as he gets older and more conventional he will also let go of any sexual inhibitions and allow spontaneous 'feelings' to enter his heart.

Pan often gets involved with women just for financial or

33

career advancement. You'll often meet rich and successful females who have been taken advantage of by a Goat. Some of them have the man tethered on the dry arid plain of a monotonous marriage, but most of these Goats are already up there at the top of the mountain. The funny thing is that a Capricorn can digest all the flack you might throw at him for using you. A Goat's stomach speaks for itself!

The Capricorn man is shatterproof and biodegradable. Once he's decided you're the partner for his tenacious way of life, then he'll want to run you as smoothly as his business.

He can seem cold and passionless, restrained and indelicate in sexual communication. He is awfully possessive and it's very hard to change his opinions. But the taciturn Goat has a dry and witty sense of humour and there's always that twinge of inner warmth to draw out. He's not dull, but his approach to sex can be as disciplined and as ambitious as his approach to work. There is a closet romantic in his heart trying desperately to get out, and he needs a wise woman to open the door for him. As long as your relationship is within the boundaries of his own white lines, and he is in control, you'll find the most loyal and reliable partner behind those wardrobe doors.

THE CAPRICORN WOMAN

Don't ever expect a romantic encounter with this woman to last very long. She'll have all those graceful, feminine wiles, make all those suggestive noises about a full-scale affair, but the kissing and the innuendos and the candlelit dinners will last only as long as she wants them to. And that is often shorter than you'd imagined!

The Goat lady is always ambitious and she knows what she wants. If she wants you, she'll look beyond the romantic aspect of love for something more stable, more gutsy and more to do with a business arrangement than an emotional one.

She is often power-mad, whether it's in the office, or in a relationship. There's no point floundering around in bed making wild romantic promises, and sharing ideals when you can go for the real thing. A commitment, a permanent relationship. She doesn't relax in love easily and has a cool approach to sex and emotions. But if you give this Goat the lead she can be intensely passionate and will gradually lose her shyness once she's known you a long time. She has to control the affair her own way, but don't let her fool you into thinking her calm and bossy approach is the only backbone to her heart and her head. Her feathers are easily ruffled and, although she doesn't live in the twilight zone of feelings, she can get jealous and brood quite easily, and sulk if she feels slighted or betrayed.

She needs to know exactly where she's going in life and with you. Self-imposed discipline makes her sometimes pessimistic and will convince her that love is as shallow as your first kiss in the back of the black cab. Capricorn girls find intimate relationships difficult to handle unless they are really in charge, and that's why they make excellent partners or wives, but not very wonderful lovers.

The Goat lady needs her home and her mountain to climb. If she is sure you are worth pursuing she'll also ensure that she is ambitious for you too. A lot of Capricorn ladies are the true reason behind a man's career success! If you can let her take the lead through the chaos of emotion, not burden her with demanding encounters and weak-willed indecision, then she'll stay at the top of the one mountain she yearns to climb with you, called love.

THE AQUARIUS MAN

You have to remember that the space-age man is an unconventional and eccentric freedom lover, and yet wants to be everyone's friend and stick to his own quite rigid lifestyle. Aquarian men set out to find as many friends as they possibly can, rather than worry about love and sex. Love and sex are valid, and part of life, but they aren't the be-all of existence for this fixed Air sign. As long as the Water-Bearer sees change and progress in others, or in the world around him, then he is blissfully happy. He does not particularly pursue or encourage it in himself.

Our Uranus man is an out-of-space man. He's an oddball, a weirdo, often the man you meet at the office disco who doesn't drink and doesn't dance but smokes a pipe and looks like an anarchist. He might also be that man on the commuter train you see every morning who gazes at you with alien eyes and has an aloof and rather cold appearance. He's actually silently working you out, because Aquarians, like Frankenstein, enjoy scientific investigation of the human psyche!

His feelings about women can be as cranky as his habits, but there is one thing he will always do first before he makes any move to attempt a relationship: convince himself that you are strong enough to cope with his inquisitive and probing mind.

He feels it's his right to know everything about the woman of his choice, and the deeper the mystery you stir, the longer you remain an enigma, the more likely he'll want to nose-dive into your secrets. So make sure your game of 'catch me when you can' involves a worthwhile solution!

The secret of the universe, your sexual appetite, you name it, the Aquarian will unravel the truth to expose the answers. Sex is no less, no more, important than any other facet of his active life, and if you're happy to consider sex and love as part of your life too, then you'll stand a better chance of a long-term relationship with this man and all his friends.

Love is impersonal to an Aquarian. He takes it and hands it round with the same degree of feeling (and that's an awfully hard word for him to say) to everyone. Don't ever think that you are special. You can be part of his life, but never to the exclusion of others. Being friends is more important than being lovers. This is how he will choose a soul-mate: sex comes second to this Air sign who lives in his head and rarely in his heart.

He enjoys sex but as for other Air signs it's fun, a mental experience, not emotional, and definitely not soppy. Aquarius is an abstract lover who will blow cold rather than hot. He'll persist until he strips the outer bark of your personality like an icy wind bares the most beautiful and toughest trees. If you're still in one piece and agree to be his pal, that is what counts. Who needs lovers, when you can have a good and permanent friend?

THE AQUARIUS WOMAN

Possessions and possessiveness are not something an Aquarian woman will even consider in her emotional or sexual relationships, particularly from her partner. Her unpredictable and unconventional approach to life is formulated from a stubborn need to be awkward for the sake of it.

She needs mental rapport, companionship, and above all, friendship with a man: someone she can talk to all night and all day, who will stand by her, be loyal and genuine and caring about humanity as well as about the individual long before she'll even consider him as a possible mate in bed or in the home. Aquarian women often live alone better than with a partner and spend a good deal of their lives independently succeeding in careers rather than in motherhood.

The Uranian girl's emotional detachment keeps her free from forming too intense and personal relationships. It gives her an open lifestyle, the chance to encounter as many friends as she possibly can. If you can be her friend and not attempt to own her or try to change her and accept that you have to share her with the world as she shares you with the world, then you may have found a soul-mate. Her apparent lack of passion can be frustrating, but her loyalty is impeccable and her stability is supportive.

Passion implies commitment and intensity, and to an Aquarian girl both are abhorrent. She enjoys sex and physical contact as a pleasurable and warm activity between friends, but she won't ever let you get soppy or slushy. If you do she'll think you're weak and pathetic, and she needs a tower of strength in her bed, not a fragile sandcastle. She can take sex, or leave it.

The essence of an Aquarian girl's love is based on her need to force herself to be different, to be an eccentric. She will, of course, have delved into your mind, wriggled out your intentions, and scanned you with an emotional barium meal to check out if you're worthy of closer inspection. But if friendship isn't in your heart, then love and sex won't be in hers.

THE PISCES MAN

If you've ever gone fishing out at sea, on the glimmering darkling patches of the ocean where the water is black and the bottom of the sea runs deeper than the height of the tallest mountain, then you'll know exactly what a Pisces man is like to catch. Often you have to climb into that diving bell, and take a powerful torch to locate him. Sometimes he'll emerge only to escape from life into fiction and fantasy. He'll often prefer to drown in anything, as long as it's drowning.

Fish men are charmingly romantic and awfully attractive

because they are such dreamers; a very different challenge from the passion of Fire signs, the mental agility and lightness of Air or the solid practicality and sensuality of Earth men.

Impressionable to the point of being blotting pads, they will see only what they want to see and cloud their incredible intuitive and psychic senses with careless indecision. Mr Denizen-of-the-Deep lives in a partial eclipse of life no matter what love-encounters throw at him. He is easily led astray by alcohol and women. The Fish will escape into shadowland and pretty dreams, rather than face the mundane reality of life. If he fails in a relationship it's simple: he retreats. For some-one who is actually quite gregarious he drifts through life as the zodiacal mop, absorbing and sensing your changing moods.

The Fish men are drawn to very beautiful and very female women. They are easily besotted by physical beauty. Being in love is a good escape from real life, whether it's with a beautiful day, a beautiful drink, or beautiful women. You can lead a Piscean astray more easily than you can get a dog to eat a bag of crisps, and you can get him into an intimate sexual relationship faster than a black-cab meter spends your money.

Sexually he is uniquely gifted. He doesn't need words or books, passion and emotion flow easily and love grows quickly in his deep cave of feelings. But Piscean men are often too far away in their own fantasy, and if you're not open with him you'll get left behind on the shore while he's diving back down into the deepest part of the ocean for the water spirits.

This half-man, half-fish is only ever half-seen. If you are prepared to embark on a sea voyage with him, make sure you've got the sea-legs to follow him to the deepest part of the ocean when he leaves you for his own lonely ecstasy.

THE PISCES WOMAN

The mermaid is half-fish, half-girl, and the Pisces girl is half-way between reality and a dreamworld, far from any logical or mental plane, in a world of intuition and feelings. She is usually poised, beautiful, and compassionate. Love and caring is genuinely felt, and she is kind and uniquely sensitive to others around her. She is the girl who sells sea-shells on the sea-shore, a poetry of emotional fluidity.

Of course this kind of feminine mystique attracts men easily, so she is usually surrounded by a choice of the best fish in the sea. There are many Piscean women who have been badly hurt by rushing headlong into romantic involvements without a thought because they really do not think. The Mermaid suffers intensely from emotional pain, and bitterness can turn her fishy scales to higher melancholy octaves. She can be led astray by the temptation of romance, or by the masks of drugs or alcohol to hide from her own passionate feelings. The Mermaid is deep to find. Like diving for oyster pearls, she will be hidden, unfathomable, and never in shallow water. Her elusive nature is vague and sometimes dithery, and she will always be moving somewhere and never be sure where it is she should be going.

Love is a touch-down, a grounding from reality and she'll fall into it as easily as Alice fell down the rabbit hole. In love she gets carried away by emotion and the prevailing moods of her lover can channel her through the murkiest waters and the shimmering waves like driftwood. Yet sometimes the physical intensity of her sexuality will produce emotional conflicts within herself and she will begin to see the man she thought she loved as just another shell on her lovely sea-shore. She is like the tide that washes across the empty bay, surfing back the shells to find the one that glistens in the sun, rather than the ones that turn to sand. She needs to belong to the sea of love, and to one man, and that man must be strong and protective, and mostly understanding.

The Mermaid often falls for weak, nebulous and gifted characters, a lover who makes love and feels as deeply as she. But together they will drown each other. The tide that carries her on to a better shore is the man who turns up the oyster bed and finds the real pearls inside.

The 12 Signs as Friends

ARIES

The Aries friend is rather like a meteorite landing in your life. Full of energy and enthusiasm for your friendship one day, the next deserting you for another planet, leaving you feeling deserted. Ariens can make and break friendships faster than any other sign. They hate being dependent on anyone and, on the whole, would rather have many acquaintances than close pals. Ariens of both sexes enjoy the companionship of men, and the rough and tumble of fairly lively and noisy gatherings, but they can be quite happy with their own company. They find it difficult to keep platonic relationships with the other sex and are not known for their reliability as friends. They would rather ensure they are the centre of attention so, if others are prepared to tag along with them, they may just be pally while the going is good!

TAURUS

Bulls of both sexes make warm and considerate friends. They need close, intimate friends rather than loose and casual ones and prefer the company of individual pals to social gatherings. They are always generous and would prefer you borrow from them, rather than owe you any favour, yet they are genuinely concerned for your welfare. They need a lot of affection and tactile communication, bear-hugs and cheek-kissing, rather than just a nod, both from friends of their own sex and platonic friends of the other. They like to feel comfortable and will make great efforts to make you always feel at home in their own nests. If you ever need to phone for help, a Taurean is just the sort of person to get you out of trouble, without getting het up, but they may take their time getting there!

GEMINI

Gemini loves a varied and lively social life. Not very reliable when you make arrangements for outings, they are not very fond of very intimate, close friendships. They prefer a wide circle of acquaintances to the serious one-to-one friend. However, they are so adaptable that they will make friends very quickly, chatter about the world and generally enjoy themselves. They can be inconsistent, and also gossips in big circles, so as a close and trusted friend they are not really reliable. Both sexes like platonic friendships, and you often find they have more true friends of the opposite sex than they do of their own. Very gregarious, but not very loyal, they also like to feel they can leave when they want to, rather than have any restrictions to adhere to. They need friends who enjoy intellectual pursuits rather than the great outdoors. But they are adaptable, and will try anything new, for the sake of novelty.

CANCER

Crabs take a long time to make friends and therefore prefer to make firm relationships with people they can trust and have known for a long time. They don't enjoy big gatherings, and rooms full of people they don't know, but will enjoy socialising if it's among

43

small groups of similar-minded people. Can be surprisingly obsessive about maintaining a close friendship and need to feel they can rely on someone to talk through all their own fears and woes. Cancerians are generally cautious about lending money, or any of their possessions, and don't particularly like being asked about their finances. Although they insist on depending on their close friends, they are also easily hurt if let down by others and can take it very much to heart. But they are wonderful at helping in a crisis, and will never let you down.

LEO

The Lion likes to roar and be the centre of attention in any social gathering. They make friends easily with both sexes and will often have a very wide circle of friends to amuse their ego-orientated heads. Leos make good friends and are more reliable than the other Fire signs. They are intensely loyal and will stick up for any one of their acquaintances if they get into trouble, or need supporting. Though not emotionally close to new friends, nor even to the old and trusted, they do need warmth and a fun-loving rapport to stay your pal for long. They are open-hearted and quite generous, but don't ever betray their trust or they can scratch back. Most Leos love socialising and parties, and are often the all-night party goers rather than the dinner party type.

VIRGO

They make difficult friends as they never quite get close enough to anyone, nor accept other people for what they are. They can be cold and judgmental, and also, once they think they know you, can seem quite critical. Yet they are good at socialising on a wider scale, and enjoy casual acquaintances and brief friendships so

CANCER

that they don't get caught up in emotion. On a wider scale they will be lively, fun to be with and enjoy intellectual and stimulating company. They are very cautious about who they invite into their house, and often prefer not to venture into other people's homes: it gets too warm! They like general chit-chat and would prefer to chat to friends in the pub and not make any commitments nor rely on others for anything. They are very single-minded but can be relied upon to organise any event or social gathering. Societies and clubs are their favourite way of keeping acquaintances around them and not getting tied down.

LIBRA

Libra is the most sociable and affable of signs. Librans love parties, social gatherings of all kinds and will always want to make friends with as many people as they possibly can. Librans are also quite a dab hand at keeping in touch with old friends, and they look on casual acquaintances with as much sympathy as they do someone they've known since childhood. Librans need a lot of company and don't enjoy the solitary life. As close friends they can be relied on, but they often have a habit of appearing interested in what you have to say when in fact their mind is somewhere else. They are not particularly deep, nor passionate about forming a close bond unless a friend is prepared to make an effort too. They love gossip and small talk, and don't enjoy lengthy philosophical discussions

SCORPIO

Scorpios are slow to make friends but, when they do, they make them for life. They aren't too fond of large gatherings, but may appear on the surface quite charming and outgoing. Underneath they are probably testing you out to see if you live up to their incredibly high standards! Most Scorpios need very close and intense friendships. Because it takes them so long to decide whether they have found a true and confidential pal, they often find that they lose friends quickly. They don't like to rely on anyone, but they will provide all the emotional support that anyone could need, and have admirable shoulders to cry on. Scorpios can usually and intuitively know if someone is a fair-weather friend but, once a bond is formed, they want it to be unbreakable and don't respond well to casual, light and inconsistent friendships.

SAGITTARIUS

Archers usually have a wide circle of friends, and prefer light and easy pals to any deep and meaningful ones! They move around so much that they are likely to make friends with strangers in the street. They are never suspicious, and never cautious and, if a friend turns out to be an enemy, they can shrug their shoulders and bear no malice, as they just move on to another one. Their open and freedom-loving approach to life makes them fairly unreliable friends to have. Although they can enjoy the company of their own sex and play light amusing games, they aren't good at any form of permanence. They don't like making arrangements and would prefer just to turn up when they feel like it. Both sexes like platonic relationships and feel more comfortable surrounded by many rather than a few.

CAPRICORN

Rather stuck in their ways, Capricorns are not good at making friends and not easy to make friends with! Both sexes prefer the company of men, and

CANCER

would rather form any relationship on a business arrangement than anything looser. They don't need a wide or varied social life and enjoy the company of a few friends who share the same ambitions or mental stimulation. Once they do form any strong friendship, they will try to keep it for life and do not take kindly to being let down. They are not particularly interested in giving or going to parties, and would rather talk in the boardroom or the pub where they feel safer in a neutral environment.

AQUARIUS

Aquarians are naturals at making friends; and keeping them. They love to have a wide variety and circle of friends, and will insist on maintaining endless platonic relationships to ensure that their altruism is genuinely felt. They are in need of mental rapport rather than any sporting or clubby basis for friendship. They are consistent and determined to supply any mental or emotional support they can handle. Although rather cold emotionally, they will always analyse friends, problems and crack the truth, rather than lead you into false promises. Although they prefer people with cranky or eccentric minds like their own, Aquarians enjoy the company of anyone who can stimulate them intellectually. They always say what they mean, and can often be awkward about your judgments. But they will never let you down in a crisis

PISCES

Pisceans are only slow to make friends as they are a little wary, for all their gregarious nature. They mix well in neutral surroundings and enjoy informal parties and gatherings where they can merge in with the crowd. They enjoy friends of both sexes and prefer to feel relaxed and non-committal rather than have pressures and obligations forced on them. They make wonderful friends when a rapport is established and are genuinely sympathetic, genuinely compassionate and always ready to help with any emotional comfort or support. They prefer a strong mental and intuitive friendship but can be too impressionable and soak up others' problems and bad habits rather than remaining independent of them. They often have a large circle of acquaintances and don't often have many close friends. Pisceans usually have one very old friend to rely on in times of trouble.

Some Famous Cancerians

Meryl Streep (22 June 1949)
Adam Faith (23 June 1940)
Carly Simon (25 June 1945)
George Orwell (25 June 1903)
John Inman (28 June 1937)
King Henry VIII (28 June 1491)
Charles Laughton (1 July 1899)
Lord Owen (2 July 1938)
Ken Russell (3 July 1927)
Neil Simon (4 July 1927)
Sylvester Stallone (6 July 1946)
David Hockney (9 July 1937)
Dame Barbara Cartland (9 July 1901)
Virginia Wade (10 July 1945)
Harrison Ford (13 July 1942)
Sue Lawley (14 July 1946)
Linda Ronstadt (15 July 1946)
Donald Sutherland (17 July 1935)
Nick Faldo (18 July 1947)
Diana Rigg (20 July 1938)

CANCER COUPLES

Business partners, past and present

Richard Rodgers (28 June 1902) and
Oscar Hammerstein II (Cancer – 12 July 1895)
Jennifer Saunders (12 July 1958) and
Dawn French (Libra – 11 October 1957)
Ginger Rogers (16 July 1911) and
Fred Astaire (Taurus – 10 May 1899)

Romantic couples, past and present

Esther Rantzen (22 June 1940) and
Desmond Wilcox (Gemini – 21 May 1940)
Prunella Scales (22 June 1932) and
Timothy West (Libra – 20 October 1934)
The Duke of Windsor (23 June 1894) and
the Duchess of Windsor (Gemini – 19 June 1896)
Mel Brooks (28 June 1927) and
Anne Bancroft (Virgo – 17 September 1931)
HRH the Princess of Wales (1 July 1961) and
HRH the Prince of Wales (Scorpio – 14 November 1948)
Tom Stoppard (3 July 1937) and
Felicity Kendal (Libra – 25 September 1946)
Michael Williams (9 July 1935) and
Dame Judi Dench (Sagittarius – 9 December 1934)
Bryan Forbes (22 July 1926) and
Nanette Newman (Gemini – 29 May 1939)

Astro Meditations

FOR YOU AND YOUR PARTNER FOR 1994-1995.

ARIES

Being first in everything is being part of everything. Use your energy and impulse creatively, spontaneously. Be you, but learn from gentleness. Fire is cosmic, don't burn others up, set them alight instead.

TAURUS

Hedonistic, jewels of sensuality. Pursue pleasures instead of waiting for them. Resentment builds on regrets. Take notice of energy, ground it if you must. Endurance is an art – respect it.

GEMINI

Seek change, but seek change within. Don't try to look deeper, you can't. The surface is coloured, is covered in shimmering. Let it be superficial, let your sexual love and lightness glide.

CANCER

Be a lunatic but face the truth that you have deeper emotions. Insecurity is instability. Sex and love can unite. Don't hide yourself from your truth – you are an introvert/extrovert. Light a candle to yourself.

LEO

Self-gratification. You love to impress, to make a noise, to have power. Power can be constructive, love and sexuality instructive. Flash warmth. Roar with pride rather than conceit.

VIRGO

Let go of the sex manual. Take a trip on surprise, on unpredictability, that is love. Stop worrying – be dippy. Perfect diffidence, it is as refreshing as your crisp mentality. Jog in bed, dissent.

LIBRA

Romance is born easily. Use charm explosively, no time for hesitation. Fall in love with love, but make it clear to yourself. Clarify romantic attraction and know it for what it is.

SCORPIO

Sentence only your obsessions. Keep others' mysteries as proof of emotions. You feel love as sexuality, as wholeness – the mystery and the answer to life. Fulfil your needs tenderly, administer with light.

SAGITTARIUS

You can expand, let others know. Give yourself freely, without blunt words. Wise to the world, wise eventually in love. Try loyalty, let go of promiscuity. Challenge sexual egotism with altruistic love.

CAPRICORN

Treat sex as an infant, nurture it. Grow with it, not against it. Try reaching out, try giving with the heart. There is no power in restriction, in restraint. Tie sex to love instead of to the bed.

AQUARIUS

Rebellion hurts others. Convention can work. Friendship is your heaven – let others come closer, let others conform if they must. Sex can be part of love, not a trap, it can be free.

PISCES

Ideals, half-seen, half-being. The stray are led astray more easily than the homed. The clouds can open with rainbows on the ocean. Take a deep-sea dive, communicate love instead of drowning.

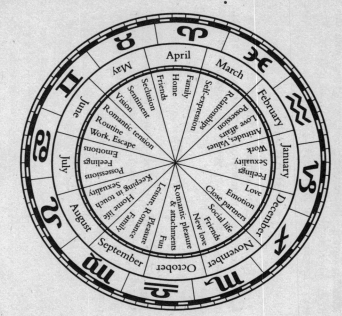

Your at-a-glance chart showing love trends for 1995

Cancer

The inner sections emphasise the important moods and trends through each month of 1995 with regard to love, friendship, partnership, sex.

Cancer

COMPATIBILITIES

CANCER MAN – CANCER WOMAN

When two Crabs meet on the beach their usual instinct is to avoid each other's pincers as quickly as possible. But two Cancerians will meet and instantly recognise the flaws in one another rather than their claws. Because they are both slow in making the first move, and only because they are fearful of rejection, it can take a long time before they actually get involved. But the qualities they both possess: of loyalty, stability and a home-loving passion only strengthen their relationship when they finally do get together. He will be more likely to suggest dinner before she does. A Cancerian girl will certainly accept, and she is quite capable of appearing as glib about it as he is, but underneath those brave faces are panicking crustacea with the chance of the Full Moon round every corner.

The Cancer man can understand this manic-depressive girl better than anyone and yet, once they decide to form a permanent bond, they can actually make each other more melancholic, and more miserable together, than they were apart. He will criticise her as a safety-valve for his own rejection, and she will grouse the same kind of remorse back at him. Crabs are notorious for picking holes in other people once they feel safe with them. Unfortunately for these two they will both suffer pangs of rejection at every cutting remark. If they find depression a way of life in the kitchen, then in the bed they may find the rejection game an even harder play than they bargained for. It might take all night for him to pluck up courage to suggest they make love, and she might crawl off to the spare bedroom to drown her self-pity in the pillow, while he lies and waits and wonders if perhaps he should offer his arms. Once they finally agree that they do both want love, rather than just sex, then they may share the security they both seek. Their problem is that because they hate to be open about themselves – two Crabs are equally evasive, equally secretive – then it might take a long time for them to find out what the other Crab wants.

CANCER MAN – LEO WOMAN

Leo women are renowned for their bossiness and their need to organise everyone else's life. When a Lion lady meets a sensitive Cancerian man she usually thinks that here is a kind, weary soul who needs organising, will be affectionate, loving and just the kind of man to have around to boost her ego. Yet she may find out to her horror that actually a Crab, for all his sulky moods and rather side-saddle enthusiasm, wants to be the leader in their relationship. The shock for both of them is that while Leo can still do the organising, Cancer will instinctively let her get on with it, convinced secretly that he is in charge. The Crab knows that the Lioness must feel that she is in control, even if he is actually running the show. The Crab man will be instantly attracted to this woman's Fiery, proud and intensely loyal goodness. For all her know-it-all attitude, she actually means well and has a generous heart, with a real warmth that can liberate even a Crab in a deep depressive sulk. She will be the one who can lift him out of depression and coax him into an optimism that is her true spirit. The Sun and the Moon are classic in their differences, the Moon moody and silent, sensitive and emotional, the Sun passionate, vibrant and glitzy.

CANCER

A Leo woman needs someone who can understand her deep sexual desires, and a Crab man does because he has the intuition and the emotional strength to reflect it right back at her. One of their major set-backs can be that he is liable to smother himself in self-pity if the Leo lady rejects him. The Leo can sulk and proudly turn frigid, like the Sun being eclipsed by the Moon, for very long periods, if she thinks his retreat into his shell is a snub against her. It usually isn't, and there is enough warmth in this relationship to make sure that the Crab and the Lion both feel secure in the truth.

CANCER WOMAN – LEO MAN

The ego of a Leo man in search of a relationship is usually the first thing that confronts a Cancerian girl, alone and vulnerable. She will play a game of elusive interest and probably be fascinated enough by his proud boasting to realise that, actually, he may not be so bad when he calms down. He is arrogant, and he is definitely convinced he knows the answer to every subject under the stars, including the deep secrets of the Crab girl. But she will remember in her deepest fears that he's forgotten to mention himself in this scenario. What she fears most is getting tangled up and then being rejected. She'll play a challenging game to seduce him, though. And because a Moon girl senses the heat that scorches the Lion's ego she knows that he might just be the sort of man she needs. A Cancer girl wants a strong, protective Fire around her, not wishy-washy dreamers who may sink her further into her depths of despair. She wants to admire a man for his abilities, for his energy, for things that are very much part of her own strength, but often sublimated by the moods of the Moon. He will find her feminine, sensitive mystique instantly loveable and his natural protective instinct and his masculine pride will find an easy scapegoat for his boasting vanity, because he knows he will be pampered, in the kitchen, and in the bedroom.

Back in the bedroom the Leo can be over-demanding and too impulsive in his love-making and the Crab lady can be too passive and emotionally wound up. If she's in one of her moods and retreats to the kitchen for solace in a Crab sandwich then the Leo's pride can be deeply hurt. He is vulnerable, actually a lot more vulnerable than he appears. The secret is that his is a stubborn belief that he is right, always right and, like the Lion, his bravery is only as courageous as the prey he is chasing. The Crab has a very tough shell of protection; the Lion doesn't.

CANCER MAN – VIRGO GIRL

Modesty and refinement walk hand-in-hand usually. One will support the other and they both work hard to carry and to share the load. With a Crab man and a Virgo girl there is a lot of modesty on both sides, and refinement from the Virgo tastes in life. They may first meet through a third party. Cancer men don't often pick up girls, and Virgo women are very fussy about whom they talk to. A Crab will as usual be extremely cautious about revealing the darker side of his nature. He will flirt his extrovert side around quite casually and the Virgo girl can be genuinely infatuated by the bright, strong leadership quality of this sensitive and genuine man. She likes genuine people, honesty and truth. The Virgo girl will then settle down to analyse the Cancerian man. After much deliberation she reaches a decision that he may actually suffer from emotional trauma, he is affected by the Moon, but she can understand why his behaviour can change with his moods. She will suggest a relationship that can be assured permanence. He will admire her for her mental and highly intellectual reasoning power. It seems she's the sort of girl he needs, a woman who can remind him of the logic behind his deep and complicated search for truth, and someone who can keep him secure and contented. He may find after a while that her analysing turns to criticism, and that her bright and fresh intellect is too crisp and clear-cut for his more emotional, swaying one. Sexually they will complement each other unless her Virgo criticism extends to the bedroom and then the Cancer will turn as frigid and cold as the Moon.

CANCER WOMAN – VIRGO MAN

The Virgo man seeks perfection in a woman. Occasionally he comes across a woman who he thinks may be the answer to this niggling problem, but very rarely. The Crab lady certainly appears the sweetest, most charming, feminine and deeply emotional woman he has ever met, but there is something he can't quite reason about her, and he does love to reason everything. The Crab girl has the same approach to life and money as the Virgo, in many ways. They both like to look after their money, and they both need to maintain a certain privacy in their personal lives. The Virgo man, however, is cold emotionally and, although the Moon girl has her frigid moments, she needs a warmth that might not be returned from this rather old-fashioned and hyper-critical man. He worries too much about his health, and the Moon woman will know every cure in the book, intuitively she will be able to sense his headache coming on, will reach for the aspirins before he's even noticed and be at his side with a port and brandy when he's got a sneeze. They both are very attentive towards each other, but the Virgo's perfection-seeking might begin to niggle her. The Crab won't be able to take his caustic comments for long, and she certainly won't like to be organised like a telephone directory. There will be many breakdowns in their sexual communication. For, although the Crab is perceptive, the Virgo can get mighty restless about being in the same bed as anyone, even the one who he thought was so perfect. He does like his crisp white sheets and the window open in the winter. The Crab will quickly retreat and the Virgo will cool down, and the sexual perfectionist might even turn to celibacy if he feels that the Moon girl has abandoned his icebox.

CANCER MAN – LIBRA WOMAN

The social Libran girl doesn't have much trouble finding men to enchant her, nor a partner among all the choices who would like to have her as their lover. As the life and soul of the party, her charm and her wit draw all sorts of signs to her, and particularly the Cancer man, who does love beauty. Again, he can be as light and flirtatious as she, and, when he first meets her, will throw in those wisecracks and loony humour for which he is better known. The balanced and harmonious girl has the gentleness and strength of the Cardinal Air sign she is. The Crab is a Cardinal Water sign and together they can blend the right amount of companionship and understanding to stay together. Emotionally the Libran is well suited for the ups and downs of the Crab's temperament. She won't judge and she won't ever criticise him when he's down. He will be impressed, and he does need to be impressed, by her level head. He never thought someone so charming and lovely could actually be so tough and so clear-thinking, so full of life and not screwed up!

The Cancer man will never rush into anything, particularly a love-affair, or a commitment, unless he first makes very sure deep inside that he is right. (Some Crab men will ring their mother to check up with her.) The only problem with the Libran is that she really is quite hasty about being in love with love. She won't dare make a commitment unless he makes it first, but then, if she does involve herself in a permanent relationship, what if she's missing out on her freedom? The Crab may get jealous and possessive because the Libran girl does need a lively social life, whether it's with men or women. This in turn will irritate her. He really doesn't have to be suspicious of anyone. Libra will always be honest and open. A Crab often finds it hard to express himself, because he really hasn't quite worked out if revealing his true feelings will lead him into deeper waters than he can handle.

Sexually they may not get on after the initial giddy infatuation. She can be lightheaded, and lighthearted about every night, and he can get too intense and emotional for her touch.

CANCER WOMAN – LIBRA MAN

On the surface a harmonious and gentle relationship that, with time, can turn into peaceful contentment. Learning to compromise is the greatest challenge for this strangely matched pair. The Cancer woman is eternally pessimistic, and the Libran man is always optimistic. However, they can both bring each other to a realistic approach about their day-to-day affairs, because extremists are linked by the Air in the middle of their differences.

The Libran falls in love instantly and really believes (each time) that it will be for ever. The born romantic will swerve through life, in a charming and sometimes arrogant manner, convinced that all women will fall at his feet in a swoon at the twinkle of his eye. They often do. But the Crab lady will be the first to be seduced quickly back into her shell by a Libran. She will retreat instinctively because she can intuitively sense that the Libran man has done this before, can fall head over heels with the surface attraction and then give up when the harmony ends and the bitterness begins. But why should it with a Cancer girl? For a start she is a home-lover, not a daytripper. She doesn't dampen personal freedom and, for her, commitment is security. The Libran needs warmth and stability, but he also needs to venture forth, to play the romantic whenever he can or he becomes stifled and resentful towards his partner. If the Crab can let him go when he wants, doesn't question him or get emotionally possessive, then they have a chance. Essentially they are both kind, and peace-loving. Arguments would only be caused by the Cancerian girl's frigidity or the Libran's rather tactless self-opinions and lack of direction.

Sentimentalists can share the past, but, unless the Crab can steer clear of suspicious and possessive emotion, and the Libran man can try to let her share his social wandering so that she has no cause for grouching, they will have little nostalgia to enjoy together.

CANCER MAN – SCORPIO WOMAN

A highly charged magnetic and sexual attraction formed from basic empathy. The Scorpio woman may realise that the deep emotional caves of the Cancer man's inner psychology are the kind she can reach, and only she alone. Both are so emotionally tuned in to each other that it is possible that they can destroy one another too quickly. The Cancer man will find her powerful personality a little overwhelming at times. She will want to control him, and not be the one to follow. However, the Cancer man will want to be in charge and this can cause the Scorpio woman to lash out when she would be better trying to understand her own insecurities. Their differences are great, but their passion will override most of their day-to-day problems. Blackness is something a Cancerian man can sink into, as easily as he can lift the clouds of depression with his laughter and mad, loony humour. These moments of madness the Scorpio needs in her life. She is known for her gravity about everything, and her intensity in everything she feels and does. This makes the Cancerian begrudging and melancholy at times because he really deserves more lightness in his own mopish lamentations.

Sexually, she will melt his side-steps into a dance of ecstasy. Not many women can really get a Cancerian man going, but this one will, and it will be a buzz he will remember all his life. One of the reasons is that they are both secretive to the point of facing the firing-squad rather than admitting the truth. But neither of them will accept secrets being withheld from them, and there could be a lot of interrogations from either side. He is possessive, she is innately jealous, and her tail can strike with alarming ease if she feels his aloof retreats from her could be anything to do with the suspicions she's cast upon him. He is equally suspicious, but her intense passion for him, or her intense rejection, will either sever their relationship completely or create a deeper bond between them. Hers is a passionate and often destructive love, and the Cancerian shell has to be strong enough to take the sting and the anger when she is slighted by his retreats. To her this is rejection, but they both fear losing.

CANCER WOMAN – SCORPIO MAN

This other Watery fatal attraction is not so disastrous as when the man is Cancer and the woman a Scorpio. There is, at the start, an obvious sexual magnetism. They both feel the same urgent responses towards one another. The Scorpio will be able to see right through the Cancer's shell. To him it is as translucent as mother of pearl and, to a Scorpio, a shell is no barrier to the one he desires. Emotionally and sexually he will immediately be able to respond exactly to the Moon girl's subtle and mysterious sexuality. Crab girls really do want someone who can understand their silence, their sensual and gentle modesty. The Crab's shy inner self will be upturned once the Scorpio man begins to penetrate her normally tough waxing. Because he is so aware of her needs she will instinctively let go of her outer Crab-like pincers and she will feel secure in his intensely hungry soul, perhaps more than with anyone else. It won't be a sensitive relationship, however, more a battle of wills, passionate and sometimes a doomed affair. Scorpios have always the problem of their destructive nature, which works alongside their constructive one. And he will demand power in the relationship, emotionally and sexually.

What Scorpio wants to believe in a woman is that she

will be as fanatical about him as he is about her. A Cancerian girl does get obsessive about love. It may only be the whole of her life for that moment, the next she may suffer the pangs of disillusion: she is a creature of changing moods, remember. Both have shells that need cracking, and maybe the Cancer girl, once opened up, will show the Scorpio that it's not so bad being exposed after all. They both suffer from pain and instability, but the Scorpio is more of an extremist than the Crab. For all her depressive lows and manic highs, he will be the one really to suffer if she ever rejects him.

CANCER MAN – SAGITTARIUS WOMAN

It's not easy for the freedom-loving Sagittarian woman to accept the gentle but demonstrative leadership of the Cancer man in her life. She would rather be doing a different kind of head-hunting than the career kind, and, for any girl Archer to admit to be turned on by domesticity and routine, she would have to held down and tortured first. The Cancer man will find her very extrovert spirit of adventure a headier version of his own manic side. For the Archer girl is the most blithe spirit of them all. She may have her faults, she may be land-locked in honest self-expression and the need to move on to another challenge, but, basically, she doesn't worry about emotion and finds it a tad stifling in her irrepressible and easy-going lifestyle. The Cancer man wants to possess and cherish, to be treated with gentleness, for his shell to be opened daily and be cleaned out spick and span with housewifely devotion. This woman will rarely even imagine being someone else's groom, but she might enjoy leading him astray for a while. She is Fire and he is Water, and usually the firework is put out quickly by this man's emotional puddles. He can turn her on sexually and induce sensuality and a little refinement to her rather casual love-making. But the passion she feels won't be enough to enliven her twenty-four hours a day.

She needs a mental and physical equal, not a secretive, wound-up Crab with a nasty chip on his shoulder about his mum. If, for a while, he seems an escapist and a lunatic, both of which she admires and is attracted to in a man, then maybe she will hang on to the extrovert side of his nature, until the Moon comes back to shadow him in melancholy. Yet he will adore her frankness, at least she doesn't criticise, only tells the truth, however painful it is. She will want to travel the world, he would rather avoid anything which requires coming out of his shell, and whether he can cope with her free love is questionable.

CANCER WOMAN – SAGITTARIUS MAN

The deep-seated devotion of the Cancerian girl can make a Sagittarian male almost retch with the thought of all those nasty words in his dictionary like chains and ties. Not that a Sagittarian is ever nasty, he is always honest, a bit of a scoundrel, and basically so happy-go-lucky that most women want to capture him. Unfortunately he is not the catching type. A Crab out on one of her sideways walks may come across such a vibrant, sparkling Archer and decide that she can't stop herself falling in love, so she might as well sit it out in her Crabby shell until he comes begging at her door. Her determination is admirable, but the Archer, in all fairness, really loves all the world, and lots of women. He prefers the company of extroverted, funny, charming, beautiful girls, to the more introverted damsel-in-distress types, but he has a very soft heart and will defend any woman in trouble, or any girl who needs a friend and a shoulder to cry on. When friendship is mentioned he's frank, forthright and blunt. He will play with the Crab girl's apparent lunatic fringe character and not realise that, in the background, her emotions are flowing towards a very deep river of sorrow, when he finally says some outrageous, cutting remark that he didn't actually mean.

The Crab will always listen to an Archer. He can go on for

hours in a rather optimistic and self-centred way. He changes the subject as quickly as a Gemini though, and if the Crab touches on emotion or commitment too soon, he will change tack more quickly than he can change his ideals. In sexual intimacy the Archer is quick to please and fired spontaneously. He would rather have sex when he feels like it. She would rather it were a routine sensual experience where true feelings were expressed, both physically and mentally.

Jealousy will be the catalyst for their arguments and, eventually, for their separation, for this man is profoundly freedom-loving and this woman is deeply possessive.

CANCER – CAPRICORN WOMAN

The simple fact of the matter is that most opposition signs of the zodiac have a great affinity for each other. It is something they can both sense but are often not sure why, and, least of all, are able to communicate. Both the Cancer man and the Goat woman are the least likely of all the zodiac to communicate verbally anyway, which makes it doubly hard for them to verbalise their feelings and desires when they first meet.

They both need power within a relationship, and this can cause a sticky beginning. The Crab is motivated by his own lack of confidence and fear of rejection: he needs to enrol a tender leadership, a sideways attack, rather than full-frontal recklessness.

The Goat lady appears on the surface a veritable kid glove, rather than a Goat, but beneath her calm and thoughtful exterior, beats a hard and sometimes mercenary ambition to run every show on earth.

Her efficiency is what makes the Crab's heart flutter with desire. Here is a woman who loves stability, is quietly romantic when she chooses and doesn't have stinging arrows to throw at his emotional side. Well, not at the outset anyway. The problem is that the Goat lady will, of course, love the initial fling of any romance, she is charmingly feminine and will provide him with the reassurances he needs. He will also provide her with the solid rock and desire for success that he would like to believe he is capable of and often dare not test out. Together they make a formidable pair, a good partnership, if they can rationalise the fact that the Cancer male will often have to play the mother figure, while the Goat girl takes the lead and ensures her climb to the top of the mountain. After the romance has faded they should still be able to satisfy each other sexually, although the Cancerian man is more likely to suffer from frigidity brought on by her apparent lack of interest. Her life is serious, and she takes sex seriously too. But she won't be pressured into false sentiment and unreal emotion. She will warm to the sexual thrill between them, and even the Crab will come out his shell. If he does the Goat may climb down from that mountain, just for a while.

CANCER WOMAN – CAPRICORN MAN

The secret desire of most Cancer girls is either ambitions for their career or their ambitions to find the man of their dreams. The driving force behind the Capricorn man's motivation is either for a strong and equally ambitious woman, for his powerful need to be on top, or for winning consistently until he proves his place in the domination stakes. Both these opposite signs share the need to lead, to be on top. But the Cancer girl is always ready to take on the support of an equal, as long as he doesn't dominate her. The Goat's hardiness, his ugliness, are actually quite appealing to the gentle Cancerian waters. She wants to build a solid home for him, to be there and support him, as long as she has her own way and as long as he is also able to accept her own ambitions. The Crab won't be that keen on the way the Goat runs their relationship like a business association. His initial romantic inclination is well rehearsed, not the plot of an actor, but the speech of a politician. He is also a grim comedian, the taskmaster, the ordered man who will only allow chaos in his life if he is in control of it. When the rather loony Moon girl enters his domain, full of conflicting emotions, sensitive and inconstant whims, he will be put to the test. To order her might be to lose her.

Both these signs need stability in their life, and their sex life will be a permanent fixture. For once the Goat may well choose to experiment, he may not 'feel' with the same depth as the Crab, but he will always be there, aware, determined to be the one to rock her bed, fascinated by the power she can exert over his hard-edged sexuality. The Crab can melt the stern face of the Goat's father-figure ways, and the beautiful Moon girl will reflect only the bright light of success in his eyes.

CANCER MAN – AQUARIUS WOMAN

The lunatic in the corner will not obviously show his intentions towards any girl. He is a flippant impressionist at times, and at others the cynical blues player. These extremes of behaviour remind the Aquarian woman that she might like to quiz this man about his inner nature when she begins to suss him out, and she will become more fascinated by his antics when he poses no threat to her quirkiness. Aquarians believe everyone should be their friends, and the constant struggle to keep all their present and past relationships going is part of their stubborn need to be different. The Aquarian woman is nosy, not with the inquisitive curiosity of a Gemini, but because she wants to bare the facts, the sordid details of life, and then, if a man lives up to her analysis, he might find a place in her social calendar. Unpredictable as ever, she is more likely to instigate a meeting with a Crab. The independent spirit and genuine friendliness of this girl will make the Crab feel comfortable and at home (which is where he likes to be immediately). He may step out of that shell just for a while and agree to ridiculous and alien behaviour. To the Crab, any behaviour which is unconventional has got to be attractive. He is often the most conventional and passive of signs when it comes to love, and this girl isn't. Sooner or later the Crab will begin to resent her blunt speech, and her inquiring mind. He has secrets that he desperately wants to keep, even from himself. To be strung up like an intellectual and emotional corpse will make him retreat fast. Cancerians really like their love and their partner's love to be exclusive – Aquarians don't. The other problem is that Aquarian women aren't too bothered about sex. They like it, sure, but it has nothing to do with love. Love is between friends, good friends; being in love is about romance, and sex, well sex is somewhere in the middle. It's fun, and fun with a Crab is a matter of luck and the Moon. Of course, she might laugh at his conventional ideas, put him into a black mood of rejection, and the termination of their relationship will seem inevitable. It usually is, unless they can appreciate each other's very different qualities.

CANCER WOMAN – AQUARIUS MAN

The more a Crab girl attempts to circumnavigate this cranky man with her ideals about home life, permanence and stability, about emotional input and sexual fulfilment, the more the Aquarian will run for his independence and resort to his full and varied circle of friends. If he met her, was fascinated by her ability to keep every secret back from him, he will be determined (for they are awfully stubborn) to find out everything he can before he can attempt to analyse forming a relationship with her. His rather aloof glamour will have attracted her initially, she can appear very aloof too. She loves his sense of fun and his rather strange behaviour which is always fighting against tradition. This is where his fixed attitude lies: not to change and rebel inwardly against the normal constraints of society but to see society and those around him change with the world. He has the conversion of others at heart, not his own. The Cancerian girl is very adaptable, she has to be because of that shifting Moon, but she is not fond of change. If the Aquarian man digs deep enough and finds her emotional responses too intense, he may expect her to give up her secrets and be as crazy about living as he is. She is serious about everything, he is serious only about his effect on abstraction. The Moon girl needs to take a position of control in their relationship, and he will certainly find this unacceptable. He needs freedom and a lot of choice in his friendships and he certainly won't be tied to commitment.

Sex is something he's always enjoyed as any other pleasure in life. He can over-analyse, and is not exactly filled with deep feelings, but he can provide the passion, for she instils in him a need to find out exactly what is going on in her private little head. Her secretiveness is her magnetism for this man, and he won't rest until he finds out what all this love and tenderness is about.

CANCER MAN – PISCES WOMAN

The perception of a Fish woman is dazzling, it's almost like the sensitivity of the Cancerian man. Both are immediately attracted to one another and will flow into each other's hearts before they even have time to think. Mind you, neither of these two does much thinking, they live in their emotions and their intuitions. The Fish girl will feel secure and comfortable in the Crab's company. He may have his swings of mood, from depressive to manic, but if anyone can understand and tolerate them, a Mermaid can. Her insight can be a shock even to herself and, though the Crab won't want anyone to penetrate his inner self, he won't be able to resist the Fish lady and her innocent sense of knowing him, without even asking!

The Crab will love her sometimes helpless, child-like

appeal, and her gregarious charm. The quiet way she can let him feel in charge is actually rather soothing to both of them, because she needs his strength, although sometimes she could do without his weaker, more depressive moments. She can soak up his emotions so easily that she can turn into a rather melancholic dreamer with him, but she lives for the moment, and does not indulge herself as much as most people would imagine.

The Crabby claws may cling a little too much at times for this very independent girl, but she loves to be needed, and her compassionate nature will hold him close to her, if he feels alone and unwanted. They both live in their hearts, and they both are quietly private together. Sexually they can find much inspiration, although the Crab may feel the Fish is sometimes too far away and too lost in her world of dreams. But then the Crab never really believes enough in anyone. His suspicious soul is an eternal battle within himself.

CANCER WOMAN – PISCES MAN

If the Pisces man surfaces for one moment he might glimpse across the ocean a strange Moon, one that rises quite slowly over the horizon. It isn't full, it's a new Moon, glinting soft light on the darkness of the black sea. When a Pisces man first meets a Crab girl he will find her own shimmering and spooky light an encompassing magnet. He will know intuitively that she will fulfil all those dreams in which he lives. Reality is something to escape from, and with this woman he can both escape and find a true and delightful relationship. She will be a little possessive, but he shines in the attention, and the need to drift like the tides of his Moon. He is restless and changeable, for he is a dual sign, and she is adaptable and driven by the moods of her loony tunes. He admires her ability to save money, and collect the material of life so that she is secure and comfortable, while he is actually hopeless with finances, and can get frustrated by her need always to keep an eye on every penny. But he trusts her judgment. He would rather let her lead than any other woman.

Their romance will be long-lived. Both dreamers, although she can wail buckets of self-pity, the Fish will prefer to retreat into the water and avoid confrontation. He hates scenes, hates emotional conflict and, if she does drop into one of her more forbidding moods, he will escape to the bath tub, or go for a long walk, or play music until he's sure she'll come back out of her shell. But he is equally vulnerable to his own mood changes. It's not so much that he broods, or breeds resentment, for a Piscean is incapable of bitterness, but he will turn silent. He prefers his own company and turns often to solitude as his true companion.

CANCER MAN – ARIES WOMAN

Another doomed but potentially explosive relationship! The Aries girl has a direct, no-nonsense approach to love. Her feelings are aroused instantly not latently or later after the flush of passion has subsided. She'll want immediate love, to receive immediate attention. The Ram girl may be overwhelmed by the Cancerian man's love of her strength and the pure Fire burning in her soul. They both have, believe it or not, the same goals in a relationship, but neither of them is remotely able to perceive the similarities, only the differences. They both want success, both hunger after a secure relationship and both want to motivate others to love as intensely as they do. Sounds like the perfect formula? Well it's not.

The Aries girl's aim for success is a sunny, bright, optimistic motivation, and the Cancerian man's is fuddled by the Moon, always melancholic, pessimistic, sadly lacking in confidence in any relationship. If the Crab is too cautious, then the Ram is too self-confident. If the Crab plays the extrovert when he first meets the Aries girl (which he usually does quite unconsciously), she will fall desperately in love with the image that he projects so well but refuses to believe he can live up to.

He will fall instantly in love with her charm and her impetuous nature. They are both outrageously jealous. The Aries girl won't cope with his smothering possessiveness, and he won't be able to understand her anger if he so much as winks his Crab-like gaze at a distant Moon girl. He will brood, she will lose her Fiery temper. Yet his need for sensationalism may draw her constantly back to his side. Aries women don't forgive easily, nor forget, but the Cancer man is such a mad, sad clown, that she might, just for once, return.

CANCER WOMAN – ARIES MAN

The Moon girl's initial attraction to this incredibly arrogant man will probably be because of his daring, independent spirit and his extremely good looks. Water and Fire don't mix awfully well, and Fire signs don't like being smothered by anything, particularly a dousing of water; it turns their red-hot passion into a sizzling black ember of bitterness. The Aries man may admit to finding the Cancerian girl's sensuality a temptation of the flesh. He may not at first care about her deep inner self that she cherishes so guardedly, nor her emotional need for a long-term relationship with a protective, dominant male. He is dominant, but not awfully good at protecting, unless he's in the middle of a risk-taking enterprise or adventure, and then he will spring to action like Tarzan. However, the Aries man is basically too reckless with money and too reckless with most things for a Cancer girl to stay around long. And equally, his honest, enterprising spirit won't have the patience or strength to play moods with the loony Moon. He may be fascinated for a while by her intensity of feeling and touch, and her deeper secrets may unlock themselves for an Aries man, but a Cancer girl's possessiveness will send him running for the first flight out of commitment. There is always a dangerous battle brewing between sensitivity and arrogance here and he will retreat quickly if he feels those Crabby pincers anywhere near him. The last thing he really wants is someone else to worry about his pennies when he'd like to go out and spend them on anything, as long as it's flash! Sexually, he'll be enlightened by her cool sensuality, but she may not be able to put up with his passion and impulsive, hot-headed love-making. Cancer women often end up hurt because they pop back into their shells when self-pity takes them out of the frontline. And, unless she is a masochist, it is often wiser for the Crab sensibly to retreat from this relationship before she gets stuck in her shell forever.

CANCER MAN – TAURUS WOMAN

The hub of a Crab man's sexuality is his need, secretly, to be mothered. Cancerian men take great delight in lying back and letting someone else take the lead, particularly if the woman they are with is beautiful, strong-minded and willing to be the boss. The Taurean woman will quite easily fall into this role. The major problem between them is they both hate making rash and impulsive decisions. In fact, any kind of decision is to be avoided and they won't want to rush headlong into commitment. It can take a Taurean woman years finally to admit she loves a man, and it can make a Crab suffer endless emotional torment to try to admit that the girl he loves is worth taking a sidestep for around his mother's apron strings.

Cancerian men can have hang-ups about their mother which carry on until they marry someone like her. Most get out of this obsession in their teens, but there are a few old ones with a mummy problem. Taurean women have all the mothering characteristics and, if a Crab can just swallow his introverted pride and communicate how he feels, then he'll be rewarded. However, sexually they are well matched – she loves sensual, warm sex and he loves emotional warm sex – there will be trouble when they both retreat over an upset. She goes off and stubbornly sits in her field and waits, he'll pop back in his shell and won't be coming out until the tide turns.

CANCER WOMAN – TAURUS MAN

The Cancerian woman will love to cook food, and the Taurus man will love to eat it. The only trouble is Mr Bull loves solid, honest simple food. Meat, chips, eggs and beans will keep most Taureans happy. The Cancer girl, meanwhile, will be into the latest fashion in food, down the delicatessen after quails' eggs and mung beans. Those weren't really the kind the Bull had in mind and insect-sized portions just don't do much for his image. Yet she could keep this affable soul quite happy if she began to understand his very basic needs. Cancerian girls are notoriously jealous, a very different scenario from being possessive. For a while these two will appear to have the same emotions, gradually the Bull's possessiveness will cause more damage than the Cancerian girl's jealous nature. The Crab girl will imagine more than is true and will often use a man's sexual performance as proof of his love. But to the Earthy Taurus, sex isn't proof of anything, let alone love. Sex is good and natural, body language lives and love is to do with stability and ownership. The Cancer girl can fall in with this line of thought for a while, but her moody, introverted side will fill with imaginary fears. Taurus doesn't really have the energy to listen to emotional wallowing. He cares, but he won't budge from his opinions without a fight. But the Cancer girl will love this man for his solidity, and he can keep her balanced when her emotions can't handle the real world.

Taureans usually respect the Cancerian girl's sensitivity, and frankly he will be impressed that she instinctively understands every need of his body. Sexually, Cancer girls usually have a need to be dominated (women's lib or not!). But a Bull is more of an affable, idle and able conqueror with an open-ended gift for inertia. His kind of domination is gentle and caring, more like a sleeping-pill than a pick-me-up. Man on top mostly, woman underneath after all, his body is doing the work, isn't that enough?

CANCER MAN – GEMINI WOMAN

Fantasising about an ideal is something the Twin girl will constantly try to enact. It stays with her as she restlessly moves through life attempting to find out who she really is. When the dreamy Cancerian, extrovert and so like her (Look, he's even flirting!), suddenly turns into this emotional and highly sensitive Crab who lies in wait for her, one day pretending indifference, the next passionate love, she might change her mind about ideals. The Gemini girl will find this all quite romantic, and possibly enchanting. The Crab might stay up all night with her discussing the latest world news, then offer to play tennis with her at dawn which, of course, is as much fun to her as spending the night in bed with him. His reason for this is to avoid making the first move towards bed, yet she will probably assume he's as detached about sex as she is. She will find his arrogance less apparent than an Aries', less infuriating than a Leo's and thus more acceptable. She hates arrogance, and she hates egotists. The Gemini girl can think he has caught himself a harem. The Cancer man will be all things to all men, if she wants to, and while she wants to. But this doesn't last long if she gets bored with your routine first.

The truth of the matter comes when the Cancerian finally puts out his grabbing pincers and tries to possess the Twins: she will immediately feel a walkabout coming on. The Cancerian will usually pout, feel desperately sorry for himself and sink into a mood of indescribable self-pity. He only asks for it if she tells him she never really fancied him anyway. It was just a game wasn't it? Geminis are honest, so are Cancerians, but the Gemini is amoral when it comes to emotion, and the Crab can only play by the depressing rules of his introverted habits.

CANCER WOMAN – GEMINI MAN

When a Gemini man spontaneously suggests dinner with the Cancer woman he's just met at a party she will, of course, be instantly flattered, but will wonder instinctively if he really can winkle out all her secrets. The Crab girl is mysterious and he will like to solve any mental or intriguing puzzle that occurs to him. It's not so much that he has fallen in love with a Cancer girl because of her emotional content, but because she poses the sort of mental challenge that he likes to meet. This may sound cold and heartless, but Geminis live in their heads not their hearts. The Gemini man does have one, but he doesn't loan it out until he finds someone who can read its Twin desires and a Cancer girl is probably one of the least likely to do so.

They will be drawn sexually to one another quite easily. Geminis are usually youthful in appearance and exciting in bed. Twins like to have fun and to communicate their sexual habits quite openly. The Cancer girl is an extrovert on the surface and so the Gemini might think that he has latched on to a fun-loving Air sign, until he comes across the weaker, emotional wreck that sometimes hides behind this charade of gregarious living.

The Crab girl will take her time to get involved with this up-front, speedy man who may zoom in and out of her life when she least expects it. She needs stability and seriousness in her life; she wants to feel comfortable with the future and with the past. She wants to belong, and the Gemini man doesn't want to belong to anyone. He is the drifter of the zodiac, the nomad of love. If commitment throws its ugly head in hearing distance of his own radar, he'll pack his bags quite happily. Sex isn't important to him, not physically, nor emotionally, only in his head. Unfortunately it can be the very existence for a Moon girl.

Cancer

PREDICTIONS
October 1994 – December 1995

♋ OCTOBER 1994

The moods of close friends and partners are never really as viable and reliable a sounding-board as your own more instinctive and intuitive ones. During the past few weeks you may have felt more involved with your very precious home life and had little social contact or little emotional connection with those around you. Your magnanimity is not something you are well known for, but your sympathy can be filled with genuine compassion if it involves close relationships. The days when you appear full of lively and practical resourcefulness are only covering up a depth of emotion that you have to tolerate alone, and at times grudgingly. However, you cherish your home and family life, and prefer the company of very close friends, than any wide hotch-potch of acquaintances, and October may stimulate that part of your nature to enjoy the quiet while you can. The new Moon on the 5th highlights the month's routines that involve both reality and energy relating to your home life.

You may be feeling dispirited now and troubled by your moody introversion but, by the end of the month, you should have regained a sense of sympathy and gentleness towards your friends and relatives. The Full Moon on the 19th intensifies your ambitions both where work is concerned and also where your relationships matter. You are not normally aggressive about what you want in life, and often you have had days when the swings in your moods can give you more depressions than you would care for, but the light that glows in your sensitive heart may be rewarded this month when, not only does the Moon make an evocative and loving aspect to Venus on the 7th, but the Sun now moves into Scorpio on the 23rd and remedies the burden of work and responsibilities, giving a little light relief. Whatever has been inflicted upon you recently where romance and happiness are concerned, you could find your emotions gathering strength at last for a new and meaningful partnership.

Your sometimes self-pitying air will disappear; you will take on a new lease of life, and those around you may even suspect you are high as a kite because of an emotional change.

<h1 style="text-align:center">♌</h1>

NOVEMBER 1994

The dreamy quality that you carry with you even in your rather extrovert moments, will follow through this month, but you should be prepared for a more lively and social calendar than you have recently experienced. The 1st reminds you that your domestic and home ties should not be forgotten, but you may find you want to express your needs and communicate your fears and anxieties of the past few months. Now, with a heavy weight and responsibility off your shoulders, your mood swing will be towards enjoyment and love rather than directed inwardly. You are both introvert and extrovert, and at times the fun-loving and lively attitude you exude on the surface often belies the deep and tormented soul that scurries beneath.

If you are already committed to a relationship, and Cancerians are always in need of the permanence and stability of a secure partnership, then this month may see a challenging aspect of the Moon and Uranus in the area of your chart relating to partners enticing you to turn the taps of social life on full, and ignore the deeper emotional problems in which you usually prefer to wallow. Partners may find your extrovert mood exhausting. If you are single you may find that this month your social life heralds the beginning of a new romance. The Full Moon on the 18th in Taurus will enliven and inspire any friendly gatherings or small groups where you feel most at home. The Sun and Jupiter, and the Sun and Pluto, make two powerful and overwhelming conjunctions at the end of the month around the 19th and 20th, when you may actually begin to understand the undercurrents of who you really are, and what you would like to get out of a relationship. This opening and expressive mood should enable you to communicate any difficult emotion both to yourself and to those around you.

The social romancing may be fun on the surface and you are as adept as anyone at the light and flirtatious approach. Yet the need to move on and to expand your interests and your emotions won't be taken lightly by close partners. You may end the month with less caution and more optimism than you have felt for quite a few months.

♐ DECEMBER 1994

After the flurry of living it up with a merry round of social activity and light romance in November you may find December brings back the memories of the introverted part of your nature. The Full Moon on the 18th may motivate your need to withdraw for solitary comfort and to inspect your psychic and imaginative energies. This in turn may lead you to stay at home and not gad about as in the previous month. This changeable and often touchy moodiness can only remind you that your marvellous capacity for pity and sympathy for yourself could also benefit those around you. As much as you seem to care on the surface, deep down your emotional content is turned inwards, rather than outwards. However, Mars enters Sagittarius on the 12th and your energies can be revitalised and put to use when you may be confronted by phone calls and demands from partners, or from a new romance, to ascertain why you have skipped social living for total solitude. Answering to the world is against your sensitive nature, but this month you will have delved within yourself enough to give answers and make statements that show that, although you would prefer to escape from reality and the world, you still require pleasure, love and harmony in your life, and a permanent place to hide.

Love could be big business throughout this month and, if you follow up a brief relationship that may have already petered out, with the Moon making a moody aspect to Venus around the 28th, you will be pleasantly surprised how someone can seem to relate to your very secretive passions, and very personal dreams, as if they were their own. Because you are now prepared to communicate feelings to loved ones as well as to yourself, for a while at least, you could find a happy rapport to keep you busy and fascinated over the holiday period. The end of the year generates not only the emotional security you need to keep your dreams alive, but also reminds you that emotional conservatism and clinging to the past is something you might have to try and change for the new and surprising year ahead.

JANUARY 1995

Your protective instincts are also the basis of the shell in which you hide the most vulnerable part of yourself. However far others can see into your hidey-hole, and however deep they dare to look, they may find there are times when even the closest and dearest of your friends cannot get near the real you. Withdrawing into the past is a way of hiding from your own suspicious mind, and sometimes the very people whom you draw on in life may seem the most exasperating when your mood changes and the introvert side of your personality relapses. The beginning of the month challenges you to take stock of all your emotional pride when the new Moon on the 1st increases a momentum, you perhaps regret having followed, towards a new or stronger emotional partnership. Close and long-standing bonds are crucial in your life, as is a safe and secure family existence. Even if you live alone, the roots, family life, from which you have left and to which you still yearn to return, are the things which make you feel content and secure. With the chance of forming a new and beneficial close tie, you may still prevaricate about it rather than activating it. And with the Full Moon in your own sign, your touchy and sometimes quite snappy introversion will spill over into your partner's and your closest friends' lives around the 16th, when you finally have to come to terms with what you love and what you cannot love. Luckily, the routine commitments and burdens of work, even if faced at home, may keep you from having to make any rash decisions as, on the 14th, Venus and Jupiter give you a breathing space to settle into your preferred secure ways and adapt gently to the thought of any change that you cannot easily envisage. With the Sun finally moving into Aquarius on the 21st, your sexual energy may be highlighted and the undercurrents of deep emotions can then be channelled into a lighter and direct route.

♌ FEBRUARY 1995

Clinging to the past can only serve as a reminder that often those dreams you cherish most can survive, as long as you try not to hang on to them too tightly and possessively. But now, February brings a brighter hope that what is yours can remain yours, and there is no one or nothing that can change it. Your friends may insist that you can become irritable and moody in the flight of the Full Moon, but this month, with your ruler in Leo on the 15th, you will feel more in touch with your own possessions and cherish the things that mean most to you, including your friends. You are not a great socialiser, preferring the company of small gatherings, and the safety of places you have tried and trusted. New surroundings worry you, and you would rather stay at home to entertain, than to go out and try every restaurant under the sun! This month you may have the chance to experience all these things. Both home, and also the lighter amusements and more pleasurable fun that you can find within your own environment should be at the top of your list. Feelings will be amiable and generally you will look upon a romance or partnership with a great deal of affection and sensitivity. You may even venture out more than usual and take time to get involved in the arts and recreations that you haven't had time for over the past few weeks. Your desire to acquire possessions may be energised around the 15th by Mars and the Moon but, with Venus currently in the area of your chart that favours close partnerships, you will be content to sit back and let others make the decisions and organise any entertainment that you are happy to go along with. A peaceful time and a time for enjoying the company of those closest to the nest.

♌

MARCH 1995

With close companions taking up most of your time, you may feel ready to drift away and escape for a while in your deeper and more intense areas of emotional security. Because you swing so precariously between extremes of gentle and caring friendliness and abrupt and snapping introversion, partners may find it difficult to understand your innermost needs and the way you relate to the rest of the world. This misunderstanding is most likely to occur around the 1st when Venus conjuncts Uranus in the area of your chart concerned with partnerships. There may be so much upset and confusion that you revert to hiding in your shell, rather than facing up to the music. There are two new Moons this month to contend with, both of which may stretch your resolve to near breaking point. The new Moon on the 1st made you realise that your ambitions to secure a safe future for your home life could be realised if you treat others with the same sympathy as you do yourself and, with the cutting Uranus ready to stir the emotional conflict, you must prepare yourself to come out of the shell. The Full Moon in Virgo on the 17th gives you the chance to communicate all your fears and woes to a cherished partner or close friend. And for once you will take the initiative and use the occasion to clarify your feelings.

Another new Moon on the 31st ties a double knot in your emotional insecurities, when you may suddenly find yourself the life and soul of a party instead of at home, dwelling on the past. The limelight is somewhere you would rather avoid, unless it is in small and very close company. The fringes of the party are fine, where you can hide in the shadows, and play the extrovert to a small audience. But with the spotlight shining firmly upon you at the end of the month, it might take you out of yourself and bring you closer to forming a firm attachment with someone you had never expected, and rekindle the truth that you have as much to lose by staying in your shell as you have if you come out of it.

APRIL 1995

The emphasis this month is very much on your circle of friends and how you relate to them. Both at home and at play you generate a strong solicitous and guardian instinct. In fact, friends and partners often find that you instil in them paternal or maternal feelings and a protective impulse that makes others feel the benefit of your company. The Full Moon on the 15th reflects the need for you to take account of your home life and to encompass your lighthearted and fun times within your close circle of friends. You may find one partner or friend behaving defiantly this month, and you may feel, as you usually do, that they are responsible for your rather negative behaviour, and therefore it is they who should be subject to criticism rather than you. But with the new Moon and Sun in Taurus on the 29th, you may feel that your social life gives you at least the opportunity to escape from reality far more easily than you had ever imagined. If to be within the company of others lessens the emotional content of your deepest self then that is where you should seek to play and amuse yourself, while the going is good. Being at the blunt end of criticism is hard for you as you take most things too personally, but you often find it easy to give. With Uranus in Aquarius now and Pluto temporarily taking a step back to Scorpio, your personal and intimate relationships should feel improved and regenerated as both your partner's and your own feelings can, for a while at least, enjoy the harmony of the social round you have encountered, even if it is very close to home. The closer to home the better for you and, if it means denying fresh enterprise, at least it will ensure you leave your moods behind for a while.

MAY 1995

The bright and sobering lights of intimate social galivanting have finally gone out and this month you begin to feel the pull of different moods, to which you can only follow and succumb. The introspective and reflective judgment of the Sun as it enters Gemini on the 21st put you temporarily in your own ice-bucket, while others are out enjoying the champagne in theirs. The Full Moon on the 14th colours your life with a richness and satisfactory contentment of your own protective and nurturing instincts. Being able to put others before yourself can sometimes be hard if it is not for your own guiltless conscience but, with a powerful conjunction between the Moon and Saturn on the 23rd, you may actually enjoy spreading your genuine sensitivity and emotional resources around your family and friends, however restrained and captivated you appear. There is little chatter in your head, the swings of love, emotional security and fun in life are taking the brunt of your changing moods and this month, although you have reached another reflective state and come out of it unscathed by the 24th, the once-unforgiving and unyielding strength you have withheld from others may be finally about to submit to your own weakness. To forgive and forget is hard for any Cancerian, but this month you may finally be touched enough by a sentiment and belief from an outside influence which will set the course for the next few months while you take stock of the true and positive benefits in your love and home life.

JUNE 1995

The Sun makes a prominent and forceful aspect to Jupiter on the 1st and, while you will feel moody and in need of solitude, there will be friends round you who may want you to increase the pace in your routines and normal day-to-day existence. To be guided suddenly out of your inward-looking self can be quite a shock, and maybe a revelation. Worrying is one of the biggest problems that you face every time any emotional conflict occurs and this month you may find that even worry doesn't have time to get activated in your mind, as Jupiter keeps you on your toes and ready for surprise. The Sun enters your own sign on the 22nd and you may begin to feel as if you are really in touch with yourself again. Your imagination can play havoc with any small niggle or word a friend has said to antagonise you. There are always words that are expressed by friends which you take too much heart. Mostly you criticise others and can't take criticism back but this month you may find that with work and routine organised and upfront in your daily existence, you cannot take time out to reflect on a relationship or partnership that seems to be hanging between a very dangerous crevice of lack of communication. With Uranus temporarily returning to the area of your life relating to partnerships on the 9th, you may feel the mood swings are from partners rather than generated by you. And as much as you would like to be in charge of the show, the very commitments and routines that have taken you away from your normal stronghold will allow the pressure to be undertaken by another. Upsets can occur and reflect badly upon those you feel closest to. It may seem that your intuition must have been misguided, but, for once, remember that it is others who should take the blame this month for exasperating your moods.

♋

JULY 1995

There are times when you would do well to think carefully and avoid listening to your intuition. As much as you would like to stand still, there is no way that the next two months are going to allow you to cling with such desperation to the past. With the Sun still in your own sign at the beginning of the month, romance and love should play in the air, and lightness may fill your heart instead of sorrow. The past must be left behind if you are to break through and beyond into a very close partner's book of feeling. They may be worn out by your mood changes and with the Full Moon on the 12th, in the area of your chart that intensifies very close romantic and personal matters, you would be shrewd to bring emotions to a head yourself, and air grievances and imagined hurts that have been brewing up over the months. Keeping such emotions hidden and then grudgingly displaying them is very much something that others find frustrating, yet this time, if you face the truth and set about restoring your protective and sympathetic instincts, then at last someone might begin to understand the real you. With a tremendous aspect between Venus and Uranus on the 28th you may feel the pull of a different and challenging relationship drift you into a new and special mood of euphoria. Creative pleasures, and the general softness of your summer fun will make the end of the month seem quieter and more in keeping with your usual home-loving pursuits. There is no doubt that what has occurred recently can only benefit your relationships with others for the future and, if you can refrain from churning over the past, and waiting on others to turn your sulks into gold, then you may at last begin to find that happiness is not just built on dreams, but on reality too.

AUGUST 1995

This month begins with the extrovert side of your nature taking full stock of the needs of those close partners and friends around you. Your fun-loving and gregarious side, when put to good use, can brighten the summer and the days with less routine and more imaginative and inspirational ideas. Leaving the past behind is often the hardest thing for you to do, your memory is always acute, and your whole existence treasures nostalgia and the goodies in the attic. Pulling them out this month may give you warm sentimental images, but there are times when you were better looking through the goodies in the present than in your past. By the end of the month communicating your fears and your personal convictions should prove that you are stronger and less emotive than you thought. Airing your grievances with friends is difficult, but this month recent introductions and distant friends may give you cause to suggest that you are visited, rather than your doing the visiting. Never one to travel far, your home will play major importance at the end of the month. You will find a new and delightful energy towards domesticity and the pursuits and leisure activities you enjoy around the home. Partners will love the closeness and the rather wider implications of your energetic desires to feel secure within the bounds of a close-knit circle of friends. The more you dream yourself into this existence though, the less you are able to face the changes that may occur from without. Your own constantly shifting moods are easily accepted at the moment, but your sensitivity to change may encourage others to try to shake off your clinging and possessive ways while they begin to search wider than the home front for their own freedom and contentment.

♋

SEPTEMBER 1995

Impressionability often lures you into new areas of life where you would rather not go. As much as you try to stay the home-loving and affectionate person, you can easily find yourself treading new water when the extrovert and fun-loving side of your personality rises over the emotional stamping ground in which you feel secure. And this September sees a month where the past is left in all its dazzling glory and momentarily you can forget worrying about reality and accept it for what it is now showing you. The month starts with a bang when Mars enters the area of your chart with regard to the gaiety and sparkle of romance and friendships in your life. Mars has an energising effect on any fun and amusement this month, and you may find that your powers of resilience to the normal spontaneity of what gets thrown your way are unable to resist the new challenges. Your normal over-sensitivity to how others see you will be forgotten and you may feel strengthened by a new, exciting relationship when the Moon makes a moody aspect to Mars on the 27th. You have been dithering about where you belong among family and friends for too long now and finally you can come to realise that as long as you feel confidence in yourself, then others will feel it too. The new Moon on the 24th sees you through the very troubles at home that have brought about a strain on your closest relationships with loved ones and, by the 26th, you should be able to devote more time and energy to others, and find a new freedom for communicating your woes.

There is much to be said for using the strength of your emotional resource to put back in its place that which you fear has drifted away. Any new partnership will hold you

OCTOBER 1995

temporarily in a mood of lightness and love, but it is the commitments to the past you have made that may determine whether you will follow the extrovert lifestyle you yearn to enjoy so much or remain in the warmth and security of family life.

The insular niche you have created for yourself may be blown apart this month, with tremendous, harmonious aspects affecting your romantic and more personal life beginning to beg attention. Now, more than ever before, you may feel ready to tackle relationships and crawl out of your emotional shell. On the surface you may be appearing more and more among circles of friends who need your life and spirit but who have yet to understand the inner tensions that remain hidden. To begin with, the first few weeks of October will carry on with your same determination to communicate and express your feelings at home. Yet, by the 14th, you will begin to find the pressure of new moods of a different frivolity inspire you to take love as it comes. A new romance, or a different attitude to a long-standing relationship, will improve things considerably around the 19th, when Mars makes a splendid conjunction to Pluto and fires both emotion, physical contact and personal love in your relationship. The explosive nature of this aspect might also lead to tempers flaring, and words being spoken too hastily, but the air that is clear after the wrath has subsided will be purer and better than you have felt for a long time. Airing your anger is a way to release all that emotional conflict within that you rarely allow to bubble near the surface. A partner who might have been slow to respond to your moody introversion finally opens up and realises the importance of your friendship and loyalty. The new Moon on the 24th will justify your need for the past week's emotional tensions, but enable you to realise that what is said is now on the table and there is no turning back. This time clinging to the past is something you would prefer to forget and, although sentimental gestures may still bring a twinge of doubt about how you behave, you may at last feel the clear air and appear refreshed to come out of your stuffy shell. The gentle and seductive conjunction between the Moon and Neptune on the 29th only serves to illustrate that, with the open and challenging punctuation mark you have put to a close partnership, your own latent, gentle sexuality is unburdened and, as ever, as faithful as you could make it.

♋

NOVEMBER 1995

Social commitments have opposed emotional ones over the past six months and, although the amount of extrovert behaviour you have found taking up your time has been a pleasure, you still would prefer at times to withdraw into your shell for a good long break from life's problems! However, this month you could still be in demand, both socially and more and more from a close and deep relationship. Friends may find your loyalty remains, but you could be drawn away more from the large gatherings and put more emphasis on solitary amusements and gentler pastimes. The Full Moon of the 7th highlights your calendar as being full of smaller, informal gatherings, where you can hold sway and feel comfortable. Attempts by partners or loved ones to pull the wool over your eyes will be best dealt with by ignoring them. Any emotional tension at this time might dampen your partying spirit for which you have developed a taste. But a series of marvellous aspects set the ball rolling for a winter of impact and pleasure, whether you prefer the quiet life or not!

A turbulent few days emotionally with a close partner involves more temper and less withdrawal around the 2nd, sparked off by well-meaning friends perhaps trying to enlighten you too much about a close romantic attachment. This gives rise to a distance you prefer to keep for the next few weeks, as a very strong aspect between Jupiter and Mars on the 16th almost knocks you off your seat and your normal resolve is turned to impulsive action and the routines you have instigated and stuck to for so long may suddenly need jettisoning for a more lively and positive response. With this kind of renewed energy and vigour you should be prepared to cope with any emotional upsets that occur around the 26th and, as Venus moves into the part of your chart related to close partnerships on the 28th, you may feel more at ease, secure and completely at one with your introvert and your extrovert moods.

DECEMBER 1995

By far the greatest challenge in your life comes when your emotional side wants to take over the side of you that respects caution in love, money and work, but also demands a busy and successful lifestyle. The moods that govern your daily life can at times turn you to melancholic moments and self-pitying tears. But yet for all that tension the Moon draws around you, you are remarkably tenacious and determined where your principles and those of others are most concerned. The beginning of December follows very much the pattern of last month, except you may retreat momentarily to reflect and inspect your inner self, which is necessary for your emotional health. Love has a way of often catching you out, of often producing imaginary fears and making you regret your past rather than activate your present. By the time you have cleared your inner self of those feelings that sink you, and your return to the brink of happiness is complete, Mars enters the very personal area of your life relating to love. Following hot-foot to allow you to communicate such feelings is the talkative and spirited bringer Mercury. This time you have no reason to retreat into the past, or into your shell, for all the odds are in your favour to take the chance and let someone very close to you understand what they are doubting is nothing to fear. You can appear secretive and tormented with guilt at your worst, and now is the time to shed light on to others' suspicions and remove their doubts as to your true desire. By all accounts a series of quite extraordinary aspects occur around the 22nd when the Sun enters your seventh heaven, along with the new Moon and the enlightening and invigorating Mercury in conjunction with Mars. Not only will you be able to express true love and devotion, to believe in it, and not be suspicious of others' motives, but you will diffuse at last the heavy clouds of tension and emotion as Mercury conjuncts Neptune on the 28th. This lightness and psychic intuition may enable you intuitively to know that love is as permanent as you had wished, and can only stay constant and dependable if you make allowances and communicate your deepest fears. To be the centre of attention in public is a Cancerian dread, but to be the centre of attention, to be wanted and loved by someone special, is the Cancerian dream. Take it now, it is waiting for you.

Cancer

BIRTHDAY PREDICTIONS

June 22nd – A year when all emotional resources could be put to the test but you find security comes with determination.

June 23rd – 1995 should herald the beginning of new commitments and promises that can only bear heavily on the past.

June 24th – A great year for you to begin to come to terms with your sensitivity regarding one particular relationship.

June 25th – Remember that your moods can often confound others, but this year forget to hide in your shell and the sun may truly shine!

June 26th – 1995 may make you realise that tenacity and caution have at last achieved what you wanted from a close partnership.

June 27th – Romance and the lighter side of living should be the focus of this year. Enjoy it, don't shrink from the limelight.

June 28th – Paths that have so far been uncrossed could soon be bridged with your usual powerful and imaginative resources.

June 29th – Love this year is something that can only grow, however slowly and carefully you try to administer your emotions.

CANCER

June 30th – A year when you can dance for once in the contentment of the emotional conflicts you have finally resolved.

July 1st – Only those who inspire you can be the answer to your romantic dreams this year.

July 2nd – In spite of your wariness to make a final commitment, this year should see you make a brave front and accept your love is cherished.

July 3rd – This year you may at last take very close partners into your confidence and, with the relief it brings, find a new haven for security.

July 4th – A wonderful year for friends and close partners to begin to understand your very introverted needs.

July 4th – You love your friends and a small social circle where you can feel at home, and this year you may feel rewarded by those who are special in your heart.

July 5th – Forgetting a former romance could be hard this year, and you may find you are put to the test.

July 6th – The home is where you are happiest and this year you should feel the stability of a loved one around you.

July 7th – The year looks set to fill you with so many amusements that you could be richly rewarded by skills you never felt you possessed.

July 8th – Long standing worries and fears may subside this year bringing a new and fresher approach to your personal relationships.

July 9th – All the heartaches you have had in the past will remind you how safe it is in your shell, but this year you will polish it and cautiously emerge like a new and sparkling Crab!

July 10th – Your life is often a mixture of great happiness and sadness, but his year you could find that all you have invested in love will be rewarded.

July 11th – However cautiously you take this year, there will be wonderful chances to clear the air and make amends.

July 12th – The year should bring you new friends and a warmth and security in any new endeavour.

July 13th – Not only have you the time and energy to look at your close relationships but, when you do you may realise how much you are truly cherished.

July 14th – Forgiving others could be the keyword this year, so make all the effort and reap all the gains.

July 15th – A remarkable year for romantic and social occasions of all kinds.

July 16th – Put your powers of imagination to good use this year and you should uncover the best love you have ever known.

July 17th – Reflect on the past too much and you may miss the year and its challenge to improve or amend a relationship.

July 18th – Although partners and relatives could be in the forefront this year you should at last realise that you have nothing to lose by feeling content.

July 19th – Begin to take loved ones into your confidence and you may be assured a happy and successful year.

July 20th – This year you should be on better terms than ever with loved ones and partners.

July 21st – Not only a year for love and romance but also for new beginnings and much social activity.

July 22nd – As each day passes you may draw more and more on your intuitive instincts to ensure a stable and confident approach to your close partnerships.

July 23rd – Only looking back now can remind you how this year you could be successful in inspiring relatives to your trust.